DATE DUE			
Jan 28 '74			
GAYLORD M-2			PRINTED IN U.S.A.

A HANDBOOK OF STYLE IN MUSIC

Da Capo Press Music Reprint Series

GENERAL EDITOR
FREDERICK FREEDMAN
VASSAR COLLEGE

A Handbook of Style in Music

By GEORGE SHERMAN DICKINSON

With a New Preface by Joan Stambaugh
Vassar College

𝄞 DA CAPO PRESS · NEW YORK · 1969

A Da Capo Press Reprint Edition

This Da Capo Press edition of George Sherman Dickinson's *A Handbook of Style in Music* is an unabridged republication of the first edition published in 1965 in Poughkeepsie, New York, by Vassar College. It is reprinted by special arrangement with Mrs. George S. Dickinson.

781
D56 L
74342
may, 1971

Library of Congress Catalog Card Number 72-90211

PREFACE

Style is one of the most comprehensive, multi-faceted, and elusive concepts of aesthetic analysis. It is comprehensive in that it refers to the work of art as a whole, as a unique identity. It is multi-faceted in that it may be used to characterize many aspects of the art work, such as period, nation, and art form. And it is elusive in that an understanding of it is not immediately evident. An understanding of style is attainable only through penetrating analysis of all aspects of the work of art and through a kind of intuitive insight into its unique character, which is extremely difficult to define.

The word "style" designates an ultimate characteristic of the work of art which cannot be reductively explained in terms of the individual factors and components of that work. Style encompasses not only components, but above all the interrelationships of the individual components functioning within the whole. Although style is something ultimate and unique, the word is flexible enough to characterize many quite different aspects of a work of art. In the case of music, for instance, it may characterize single works, composers, types of composition, media, methods of composition, nations, periods, and so forth.[1] Thus one can speak of Beethoven's style, of the symphonic style, of the French style. The most general meaning of style appears to be: that which uniquely characterizes something and defines its individual identity.

The founder of modern music style analysis was Guido Adler.[2] Adler placed the concept of style at the very crux of aesthetic analysis, making it the foundation for all theoretical and historical inquiry. He defines style as the manner in which the artist expresses himself, the manner in which the artist gives form to his moods and thoughts. This definition of style is "modern" in that it

---

[1]See Willi Apel, *Harvard Dictionary of Music* (Cambridge: Harvard University Press, 1944), 714, 832.
[2]*Der Stil in der Music* (Leipzig: Breitkopf & Härtel, 1911).

is bound to the theory of art as self-expression. Adler quotes Goethe's observation that style is a source of knowledge of far more profound truth than that obtainable by mere sense observation and sense imitation. Although an understanding of style can never be divorced from purely sensuous experience, it can also never be explained in terms of sense experience alone. Nor can style be understood through a merely "rational" explanation of forms and principles. Style is akin to the ethos, to the essential "flavor" of the work of art.

One of the most fundamental and most difficult problems with regard to the concept of style lies in the dichotomy prevalent in most aesthetic matters: the dichotomy of the subjective and the objective aspect of art. Adler understands the objective aspect of style as the conditioning factors operative in the composer's historical position. These factors belong to the organic development of music and constitute a historical influence from which no composer is totally exempt. For Adler, the subjective aspect of style consists of the individual temperament and disposition of the artist. Both aspects of style, the objective and the subjective, are always present.

The problem of style has always been central to George Sherman Dickinson's thought, and the *Handbook of Style in Music* represents the culmination of a lifetime of thinking, teaching, and writing about the concept of style. Style is treated not only in terms of a consideration of its concrete manifestations in music literature, but above all, in terms of an original analysis of the most fundamental elements of music: melody, rhythm, harmony, structure, texture.

This kind of analysis of the fundamental elements of music is perhaps one of Dickinson's two most distinctive achievements. The analysis and definition of basic elements of music such as rhythm and melody is a formidable task, and not one which he undertakes with the aid of any external viewpoint of preconceived aesthetic principles. The principles which he defines and analyzes are not principles imposed upon music, they are principles *of* music, and they could have arisen only from a thorough and penetrating study of the music itself. At the end of the Preface he cautions the reader that "constant reference of the topics and ideas of the *Handbook* to actual music is important."

The formulation of these principles is achieved, to a great extent, through a terminology which Professor Dickinson developed himself. His terminology in many instances is not merely a terminology, but the formulation of a new concept in style analysis, e.g., "analogy," "aesthetic pace," "intensity-tensity-detensity." The first two terms were developed in two earlier essays: "Analogical Relations in Musical Pattern"[3] and "Aesthetic Pace in Music."[4] Analogy is the manifestation of an organic force of great vitality inherent in the relation of pattern, the unfolding fabric of music. This organic force lies in the relation of analogue to original, in the association between a given structural unit and a succeeding unit or units, so formulated as to display similar but significantly differentiated characteristics. Analogy is to be found in both linear and polylinear music. In linear music it is an indispensable support of the extensive design of homophony. In polylinear music it forms the nucleus of the compactness native to the intensive design of polyphony.

The concept of aesthetic pace is closely related to that of intensity-tensity-detensity. The range of tensity extends from a maximum detensity to a maximum intensity, with gradations between these two ideal extremes. The two basic polarities of aesthetic pace, the lyric and the dramatic, are thus characterized by detensity and intensity. The lyric, as the creation and sustension of a unified introspective mood, is by its very nature detense; whereas the dramatic, which involves the assertion of strong extrospective mood contrasts, incorporates a strong degree of intensity. The lyrico-dramatic, the fertile hybrid of the two, combines the stability of the lyric with the restlessness of the dramatic, thus offering the fullest mutual interaction with a resultant heightening of aesthetic pace.

The second distinctive achievement of the *Handbook,* and of Dickinson's thinking in general, is his treatment of the dichotomy of the subjective and objective aspects of music. The subject-object dichotomy is a problem in all modern experience and knowledge, in the broadest sense of that word. In aesthetics this problem receives a new dimension, since aesthetic experience cannot be equated with cognitive experience, although it is in its

[3]*The Journal of Aesthetics and Art Criticism* XVII/1 (September 1958), 74–84.
[4]*The Journal of Aesthetics and Art Criticism* XV/3 (March 1957), 311–21.

own unique way also "cognitive." Aesthetics must still deal with the problem of the relation of the perceiver and what he perceives. The new dimension that art adds to the question of the subject-object dichotomy, the dimension beyond pure cognition, entails something akin to individual response or feeling and accounts for the seemingly irradicable differences between individual judgments of the work of art. The settlement of questions as to whether something is true or false requires some kind of objective criteria upon which nearly everybody can agree. It is far more difficult to find criteria upon which to base a universally convincing judgment of the art work. The work of art is not "true" or "false" in the ordinary sense of these words. It is great or mediocre or trivial, and considerations of this problem often tend to be resolved in the comforting asylum of individual taste.

In music the subjective-objective dichotomy becomes (a) more complex, and (b) atypical and less sharp. It is more complex because three, not two, factors are involved: the composer (and his system of notation), the performer(s), and the listener. It is atypical and less sharp because in music there is no "object" involved in the usual sense of that word. The ear, unlike the eye, does not objectify.

What is unique about Professor Dickinson's treatment of this problem is that he *starts* with the full *phenomenon* of heard music. This simply obviates the subject-object dichotomy. The word "phenomenon" means literally "that which shows itself." In the case of music, phenomenon could be transposed to mean "that which sounds, that which is heard." This meaning presupposes and includes the composer, the performer(s), and the listener whom Professor Dickinson elevates to the level of what he calls "the optimum perceiver" in order to guarantee the most sensitive and least inconstant listener possible.

In the beginning of the *Handbook*, the unified phenomenon of heard sound is analyzed into the two complementary phases of style: pattern and expressive effect. Pattern, the supposedly "objective" side of music, "exists objectively only in the symbols of notation in the composer's score, and these symbols are not definitive." If one wants to "locate" pattern, to find where it is manifest, one would find it at the level of heard tones-in-motion in the perceiver's imagination. The perceiver's response to this pattern constitutes its expressive effect. In other words, the real phenomenon of music lies not in the symbols of notation, which are a kind of approximation, but in the synthesizing listening process accomplished by the (optimum) perceiver. "In this experience, pattern and expressive effect become a single individual entity—the *style identity* of the particular work." Thus Professor Dickinson defines style as "the reflection of the individual essence of a work of art which gives it its *identity*." Style is defined as the unique identity, composed of the two inseparable factors of pattern and expressive effect, which is unfolded in the distinctive aesthetic experience.

The intention of the *Handbook of Style in Music* is to present (1) a method of thought about music, and (2) a tool in the aid of style analysis and criticism. In its second function it offers a rich historical spectrum of concrete applications of style analysis. In its first function it provides a uniquely original contribution to musical aesthetics: an explication of the concept of style resulting in an articulated method of thought about music.

Joan Stambaugh

Vassar College
April 1969

A HANDBOOK OF STYLE IN MUSIC

A Handbook of Style

IN MUSIC

By GEORGE SHERMAN DICKINSON

Professor Emeritus of Music, Vassar College

VASSAR COLLEGE

POUGHKEEPSIE · NEW YORK

1965

PUBLISHED WITH THE ASSISTANCE
OF A GENEROUS GIFT FROM
BERNARD M. AND MILDRED GOLDSTEIN KAYDEN
AND WITH A GRANT FROM
THE LUCY MAYNARD SALMON FUND FOR RESEARCH
OF VASSAR COLLEGE

To My Wife

BESSIE McCLURE DICKINSON

CONTENTS

NOTATION OF THE HANDBOOK

I.
A.
1. a.
  (1) (a)
    1. a.
      (1) (a) ·
        1' a'
          1' a'
	System of notation in the topical organi-zation of the *Handbook*

I. A. *1. a.* *etc.*	Used for enumerations separate from those of the main topical organization, and for subdivisions under the sign ¶.
¶1 ¶2 *etc.*	Indicate definitions, explanations, comments, etc.
I II *etc.*	Indicate movements in cycles.

SYMBOLS & ABBREVIATIONS

[ ]	Indicate references to topics of the *Hand-book*. Many of the references in the text are forward references, directing the reader to related material not yet considered.

Italic	Is used largely for analysis throughout the *Handbook;* it is used comparatively infrequently for emphasis.
. . .	Refers to intermediate graduations between the extremes given (e.g., Intense . . . Detense).
/	Indicates that the factors (or factor) following the sign are intrinsic to the initial factor of the succession (e.g., *Melody/*rhythm/dynamics/structure).
F S M	Refer to fast, slow, moderate tempos of movements in cycles.
S-F S-F	Indicate, through the hyphen, the conjunction of movements in cycles.
S F S F	Indicate, through underlining, single, double, triple, the relative intensity of movements in cycles.
T D S$_D$	Signify tonic, dominant, subdominant.
S$_T$ M S$_M$	Signify supertonic, mediant, submediant.

TERMS

The following terms call for early definition, in the senses in which they are used in the *Handbook:*

Progression Refers to the primal energy inherent in pattern which imparts to music the quality of advancing motion. [5]

Intensity Refer to qualitatively opposed degrees of
Detensity activity in progression under the general attribute of *tensity.* [5c(7)]

Linear Refers to the line of advancing motion in melody and structure, (the "forward" or so-called "horizontal" aspect of progression.) [5a(3e); cf. 4a(4b)]

Polylinear Refers to the combination of interassociated lines (as in polyphony, etc.)

Pattern Refers to the process of relating tones in time, with aesthetic intent, in the formulation of a succession of structural events. [2a]

Structure Refers to the linear or polylinear consequence of the process of pattern. [4c¶3]

Form Refers to a particular, usually conventionally accepted, version of structure, i.e., a particular form or form-type (e.g., the sonata-form). [4c ¶3]

Design Refers to the comprehensive principle of rational aesthetic order which governs the progression of the pattern and expressive effect and hence the style of the work as a whole. [10-11] ("Form," as distinguished from "a particular form,'' is sometimes used, though not here, in the sense just given to design.) [4c¶3]

Other terms are merely suitable English words or phrases in basic meanings, appropriated as technical terms for the purpose of this essay, (e.g., orientation, analogy, integration, etc.).

Various terms are explained throughout the text in statements marked by the sign ¶.

Further terms and information may be found in the *Harvard Dictionary of Music*,[1] or in other dictionaries.

The INDEX OF CHIEF TOPICS AND IDEAS, pp. 95ff, offers a useful conspectus of a large part of the terminology of the *Handbook* and of the classification of ideas represented by the terms.

[1] Willi Apel, *Harvard Dictionary of Music*, Cambridge, Mass., 1957.

FOREWORD

This *Handbook of Style in Music* is meant to be regarded both (1) as an analysis, description, and systemization, of the characteristics of style—in effect, a method of thought about music; and (2) as a tool in the aid of style analysis and criticism. In the first capacity, the *Handbook* constitutes an aesthetic epitome of the nature of the musical phenomenon as manifested in style; in the second capacity, it forms a memorandum of the evidences of style for selective application in style analysis and criticism. The fullness of detail in the *Handbook* suggests that much of the material presented may be expected to serve chiefly as background or context to the particular material selected for a given study or critique, though the study of a single aspect of style may employ the full detail. [40a] Observe that the absence of a number of traits of style in a given case may be as indicative as their presence.

The synopsis-outline form has been taken instead of continuous literary exposition, since it affords at the same time the advantage of extensive detail in organized, compact form, and of wide overview of the assembled phenomena of style. The basic principles of the art and the essential nature of the perceiver's response do not change from epoch to epoch, even amid changing attitudes. An attempt has accordingly been made to make the *Handbook* both broad enough and minute enough to cover substantially any of the styles of Western music, in which the presence of some sort of tone system is discernible. [3b(1b)] It is evident, however, that there is an elusive fringe of style not touched by any form of analysis, but reached only through sensitive, direct musical and aesthetic insight.

The interlocking scheme among various topics of the *Handbook* involves some intentional repetitions. Other pertinent repetitions are obviated by the use of references. Musical works have been cited only when confirmatory illustrations have seemed essential. Constant reference of the topics and ideas of the *Handbook* to actual music is important.

ACKNOWLEDGMENTS

The basic study of style in music, to which later studies are indebted, is: Guido Adler, *Der Stil in der Musik*.[2] Other specific obligations are recognized in footnotes.

Helpful suggestions received from Dr. Otto Kinkeldey, Professor Emeritus of Musicology, Cornell University, Dr. Paul Henry Lang, Professor of Music, Columbia University, Dr. Carl Parrish, Professor of Music, Vassar College, Dr. Glen Haydon and Dr. William S. Newman, Professors of Music, University of North Carolina, and unfailing encouragement and extensive assistance given by my wife, to whom this book is dedicated, are very gratefully acknowledged.

G. S. D.

Chapel Hill, North Carolina
February 9, 1964

After the author's death the completed manuscript of this book was put through the press by the untiring effort of his friends Dr. Carl Parrish and Dr. Joan Stambaugh.

With gratitude,

Bessie McClure Dickinson

---

[2] Guido Adler, *Der Stil in der Musik*, Leipzig, 1911, 1. Buch, *Prinzipien und Arten des musikalischen Stils*. Reissued in 1920 under the latter title alone.

A HANDBOOK OF STYLE IN MUSIC

I. The Concept of Style[3]

1. STYLE AS IDENTITY

a. Style is the reflection of the individual essence of a work of art which gives it its *identity*. This identity is the result of a distinctive *conjunction* of components, coupled with distinctive *emphases* among the components.

b. Style is thus the crystalization of the traits of a work, characteristically adjusted in one comprehensive individuality—the creative personality of the work.

¶1 Mannerism is idiosyncracy of style reduced to conventionalized formula.

c. Style is the product of the intersection of time, place, and creative temperament, working within the frame of the nature of the art. [21a]

2. THE COMPLEMENTARY PHASES OF STYLE

¶1 Style reveals two complementary phases, according to the angle of view, namely, *pattern* and *expressive effect*. This seeming duality is resolved in the integration of style which takes place in the actual aesthetic experience of the perceiver. [8]

[2 a. *Pattern*

¶1 Pattern refers to the process of relating tones in time, with aesthetic intent, in the formulation of a succession of structural events; see TERMS, p. x.

¶2 Pattern is the imaginative ordering of the mutual relations among the components of style.

[3] Cf. James S. Ackerman, "A Theory of Style," in *The Journal of Aesthetics and Art Criticism*, Spring 1962.

(1) The relations inherent in pattern are manifested in tones-in-motion in the immaterial field of "musical space" in the perceiver's imagination. [5a(3)]

(2) Pattern exists objectively only in the symbols of notation in the composer's score, and these symbols are not definitive. [14]

(3) Pattern is released from its static and objective state through the interposed agency of interpretative performance. [15-16]

b. *Expressive effect*

¶1 The response of the perceiver to the pattern constitutes the expressive effect of the musical work, or, less precisely, its "expression." [7-8-9]

(1) The complex of patterned tones-in-motion is synthesized in the immediate and concurrent response of the perceiver, and is cumulatively recreated in his musical imagination.

(2) Each perceiver is thus immersed in a distinctive aesthetic experience for each work each time it is heard.

(3) In this experience, pattern and expressive effect become a single individual entity—the *style identity* of the particular work. [10]

[2b (4) Through the perceiver's experience, a nominal form of communication is established from the composer to the perceiver [9]—nominal, because the composer's concept of the work is not likely to be identical with that of the performer, or with the perceiver's experience.

(5) In any case, the perceiver is an inconstant factor. Hence pattern and expressive effect approach a relatively ideal state only in the conception and experience of the "optimum perceiver." [18d]

[2c The comprehensive concept of style embraces all of the aspects of the complex of pattern and expressive effect. These aspects are gathered together as the *design* of the work; see TERMS, p. x; [10b, 11]

4

II. The Complementary Phases of Style

A. *Style from the Viewpoint of Pattern*[4]

3. THE PREMISES OF PATTERN

¶1 A sense of the general intelligibility of pattern, and spontaneous response to it, are assured only by the presence of preunderstood, readily recognizable concepts of pitch and time relation in the consciousness of the perceiver. These are the *premises* of pattern, more or less common to many styles and inferable from the music of any style for that style. In the case of styles whose premises have not been assimilated (and in the case of exotic musics), the perceiver will have to attempt to build up the necessary familiarity in the course of experiencing the style and by analysis of it. The premises of pattern, in its several aspects, are as follows:

[3 a. The *dimensions* of pattern in the field of progression; see [5a]

¶1 The dimensions of pattern are traversed in the field of progression. [5a]

(1) The pitch dimension (measured in intervals) [3b (1)]

(2) The time dimension (measured in beats, accents, and units of pattern) [3b(2)]

(3) The dynamic dimension (measured in approximate degrees of sound intensity) [3b(3); 5a(1b)]

¶1 This three-dimensional complex of motion progresses into a fourth linear dimension, namely—

[4] See the author's *Pattern of Music.* Poughkeepsie, New York, Vassar College, 1939.

5

(4) The dimension of structural extent (measured quantitatively by temporal length, but qualitatively by the pattern of tensities, to form aesthetic length) [5a(4c)]

(5) Color refers to three different concepts which must be properly distinguished:

(a) Color: organic color (the character of a tone combination, entering the field of progression in the dimension of pitch) [3b(4a)*7*)]

(b) Color: chromaticism (the presence of tones foreign to the mode; enters the field of progression as an aspect of melody or harmony) [4a(1e)*2*; 4b(7b)*1a(2b)*)]

(c) Color: tone color or timbre (a property of tone, with no separate dimension of its own in the field of progression) [3b(5)]

[3 b. The *vocabulary* of pattern

¶1 From the large number of possible pitches a limited number of pitch constellations or pitch-classes is taken for musical use. In tone relations the nominal central tone of each pitch-class is the nucleus of the class, though other members of the class may represent the essential pitch under varying circumstances; see [15d(1); 5c(1a)*3a(3)*¶1]

¶2 The vocabulary of pattern consists in a number of systems of tone relation, established in practice in various styles, and serving as one of the premises of intelligible pattern.

(1) Pitch relations underlying vocabulary

(a) Principles

1. Measurement of pitch: in intervals or their approximation

2. Point of reference: the tonic or final, or other demonstrated or assumed focus [5c(1)]

3. Conventionalization of pitch relations in systems (scales, modes, or other sets of relation) as bases of reference

[3b(1a)*3*

¶1 A scale is a system of tones arranged in the order of ascending or descending pitch. It may be orientated [5c(1a)

6

¶1-3] in a specific mode (e.g., the scale of the major mode), or it may be an unorientated gamut of tones (e.g., the general diatonic scale, the general duodecuple scale).

¶2 A mode is an orientated system of tones, related to one another through their relationship to a tone of reference, and, when arranged scalewise, displaying more than one different interval of succession. Each mode has its own distinctive formation, and quality or ethos.

¶3 Key is the pitch of scale or mode, designated through the tone of reference. Key is often considered to carry with it the entire relational system of the tones of a scale or mode.

[3b(1) (b) Tone systems

1. The modal systems and their inflections

a. Modality (pentatonic modes, the Greek modes, the 12 modes of Glereanus)

¶1 The 12 modes referred to are the 6 authentic and 6 plagal modes, and their transpositions, wherever and however used. (Although not always so referred to, the transpositions of these modes may be properly designated as modal keys.)

b. Concentric modalities (different modes associated with the same tone of reference)

c. Chromatically expanded modality (the incorporation of one tone or more foreign to the mode; cadential *musica ficta* is not in this context chromatic)

d. Modal-tonal hybrids

e. Tonalized modality (modes with imposed tonal orientation)

f. Pan-modality (the diatonic gamut with shifting or indecisive modal orientation)

2. The tonal system and its inflections

a. Tonality (major and tonal minor modes, and their transpositions, i.e., keys) (observe the presence of mode in tonality)

b. Concentric tonalities (different tonal modes associated with the same tone of reference)

7

c. Chromatically expanded tonality (the incorporation of one tone or more foreign to the mode)

d. Attenuated tonality (pentatonic modes, the Scriabin mode, etc.)

e. Polytonality (simultaneous tonal modes)

f. Pan-tonality (the diatonic gamut with shifting or indecisive tonal orientation)

g. Tonalized dodecaphony

   3. The amodal systems (atonal in application)

a. Sextuple amodality (the 6-tone or "whole-tone" gamut with floating orientation)

b. Duodecuple amodality, pan-chromaticism (the 12-tone gamut with floating orientation)

c. Serial or tone-row amodality (12-tone gamut with tone-row orientation)

¶1 Cf. serial rhythmic structure [4c(2h)*6*]

4. Micro-tone systems (involving systematically used intervals of less than one-half tone)

5. Exotic, fragmentary, or faintly defined "tone systems"

[3b (2) Time relations underlying vocabulary

    (a) Principles

1. The flow of time is articulated in beats.

2. It is psychologically impossible to perceive the beats of a succession as exactly equal in emphasis.

3. Fluctuation of the attention tends to throw certain beats into relief over others, i.e., to induce accent.

4. The unit of motion (the essential beat-unit, regardless of subdivision) governs temporal pace.

5. Measurement of time: in accents and units of pattern; see *6-7* below; [5a(2e)]

6. The moment of reference: the accented beat

7. Types of accent

a. Agogic accent

(1) Emphasis through slight lengthening of a beat

(2) Such emphasis is interpretatively imposed.

b. Tonic accent

(1) Emphasis through rise of pitch

(2) Such emphasis is inherent in the tensity of rising pitch.

c. Pattern accent

(1) Emphasis through initial or other prominent position in the tone-group

(2) Such emphasis is inherent in the shape of the pattern itself.

d. Dynamic accent

(1) Emphasis through greater intensity of tone (loudness)

(2) Such emphasis is interpretatively imposed.

e. Rhetorical accent

(1) Selective emphasis through dynamic and/ or agogic accent

(2) Interpretatively superposed on other accent, or—

(3) Inherently substituted for non-accent and usually reinforced dynamically and/or agogically (as in syncopation)

8. Conventionalization of time relations in systems (measure, meter, or other grouping) as bases of reference

9. Temporal pace (governed by the rate of the unit of motion)

[3b(2) (b) Time systems

¶1 Fluctuation of attention is governed and accent placed by the character of the rhythmic pattern which overlaps and incorporates the beats. [3d(2d)] The result, by inference, is a time system which tends to persist, unless displaced by another rhythmic pattern. The time pattern both produces and is bounded by the frame of the time system.

1. Declamation (associated with language)

    a. Prose declamation

    b. Poetic declamation

2. Measure systems (grouping of time units by notation, formula of longs and shorts, and/or pattern, not necessarily by accent)

[3b(2b)*2*]   *a.* The rhythmic modes (6 formulae consisting of various groupings of longs and shorts)

    b. The mensural system (division of a maximum unit into 7 progressively smaller divisions, by either triple or duple subdivision)

    c. Mixed measure (alternation of two or more measures)

    d. Polymeasure (simultaneous different measures)

3. Semi-meter

4. Metrical systems

¶1 Meter is based on the periodicity of attention and on the fact that a periodicity once set up tends to persist. Periodicity responds and accommodates to duple or triple grouping and within limits to different rates of pulse, according to the stimulus of the pattern.

    a. Meter (grouping of time units by the regular recurrence of dynamic accent)

        (1) Simple

            (a) Duple (e.g., 2/4)

            (b) Triple (e.g., 3/4)

        (2) Compound

            (a) Duple, subdivided into duple or triple (e.g., 4/4=2+2, 6/4=3+3)

            (b) Triple, subdivided into duple or triple (e.g., 6/4=2+2+2, 9/4=3+3+3)

            (c) Quintuple, subdivided into duple and triple (e.g., 5/4=2+3 or 3+2)

            etc.

        (3) Temporary change of beat grouping (change of diaeresis, e.g., hemiola)

b. Staggered meter (the systematic incidence of accents of different weight simultaneously in different lines of the texture, e.g., $< \cdot - \cdot)$
$$\cdot < \cdot$$

c. Mixed meter (systematic alternation of two or more meters)

d. Prose meter (irregular succession of different meters, laid off by accents)

e. Polymeter (simultaneous different meters)

[3b(2) (c) Distinctions in duration

1. Range of distinctions: Legato . . . Staccato

2. Graduations within the range are susceptible to close differentiation.

3. These distinctions are inherent in the musical idea and tinge the pattern.

4. They are imprecisely notated and are dependent on performance.

5. Elements of dynamics and timbre are associated with duration distinctions.

(d) Rhythm

1. Rhythm is the patterned organization of the time flow within the frame of a time system. [3b(2b)]

2. Rhythm is the embodiment, *at the level of pattern,* of the entire time organism of tones-in-motion in melody, texture, and structure. [4¶3]

¶1 The particulars are treated under melody/rhythm [4a (2)], texture/rhythm [4b(3b, 8f)], and structure/rhythm [4c(1d)].

[3b (3) Dynamic relations in vocabulary

(a) Principles

1. Measurement of dynamics: in approximate degrees of sound intensity

2. Use of signs and words to suggest relative changes of intensity

3. Pronounced dependence on performance

(b) Dynamic systems

1. Declamatory nuance (associated with language)

2. Fluctuating nuance (governed by pattern and mood)

3. Terraced dynamics (associated particularly with baroque practice)

4. Absolute dynamics (an expressionistic practice controlled by instrumentation)

(c) Dynamics as a dimension of pattern energize accent [3b(2a)7] and contribute to differentiating the lines in textural perspective [4b(4)].

[3b (4) Tensive relations in vocabulary

¶1 The line of distinction between consonant and dissonant combinations has shifted from time to time in the history of music, according to the tensity imputed to them (see (a)*4* below), and according to the prevailing tensive system (see (b) below). The distinction and terminology of (b)*2b* continue nominally in effect, even under the conditions of the system of (b)*3a.*

¶2 The tensity of consonance and especially of dissonance is reinforced by the presence at the same time of dynamic and/or rhythmic emphasis.

(a) Principles

1. Measurement of tensity: in approximate degrees of interval tensity

2. Interval of reference: the octave (in Western music)

¶1 Despite the basic function of the octave, the 5th may be considered to have equal importance as the interval of reference; cf. "stretching the octave."[5]

3. The absolute, graduated acoustical scale of consonance-dissonance (based on the ratios of the vibration rates of the component tones; qualified by equal temperament)

[5] See Mieczyslaw Kolinski, ''A New Equidistant 12-tone Temperament,'' in *Journal of the American Musicological Society*, vol. 12, nos. 2-3, Summer-Fall 1959, pp. 210-214.

4. The relative, psychological scale of consonance-dissonance (based on the degree of fusion among the component tones.[6])

5. Conventionalization of tensive relations in systems by usage

6. Resolution from the intensity of dissonance to—

    a. The detensity of consonance (cf. modal and tonal styles)

    b. The tensity of less dissonance (cf. amodal styles)

7. Tensity as organic color

    a. Organic color is the individual character of a simultaneous combination of tones of different pitch (i.e., intervals, chords, etc.)

¶1 Differentiate from tone color. [3b(5)]

    b. Each organic color has its own pattern of pitches as the basis of its distinctive quality.

    c. Organic color ranges over the consonant-dissonant scale of tensities. [3b(4)]

    d. Organic color combinations are tinged by different dynamic balances among their tones, and by the spacement and distribution of the components, without impairment of their organic character.

    e. Organic color combinations are tinged by the timbres involved [3b(5)], without impairment of their organic character.

[3b(4) (b) Tensive systems

    1. Total consonance

    a. Perfect consonance (unison, 4th, 5th, octave)

    2. Consonance-dissonance

    a. Consonance, with intrusions of incidental dissonance (consonances: unison, 4th, 5th, octave; dissonances: 3rd, 6th; 2nd, 7th, occurrence as harmonic intervals limited)

[6] See Robert M. Ogden, *Hearing,* New York, 1924, pp. 121-149.

13

b. Consonance, with rhythmically and harmonically controlled dissonance (perfect consonances: unison, 4th, 5th, octave; imperfect consonances: 3rds, 6ths; dissonances: 2nds, 4ths, 7ths) (Distinction between the perfect 4th as a consonance and as a dissonance in this system depends on context.)

c. Color consonance-dissonance (the consonant-dissonant color complex, free of resolution; cf. impressionistic practice)

[3b(4b) *3.* Total dissonance (in the aggregate, even though occasional component intervals may be consonant)
  a. Dissonance, with greater dissonance "resolving" to lesser dissonance

[3b (5) Tone color or timbre relations in vocabulary
¶1 Distinguish from organic color [3b(4a)7]

(a) Tone color is the distinctive quality of tone produced by a given medium (instrument or voice), as a result of its particular acoustical and mechanical characteristics.

(b) Tone color enters into pattern as a part of tones of different pitch and has no separate dimension of its own in the field of progression. [3a(5)]

(c) Tone color relations are the result of combining the different timbres of instruments and/or voices (instrumentation).

(d) Tone color relations are usually indicated by the composer and are subject to interpretation in performance.

(e) Tone color enters expressive effect as a part of the sensuous impact of tones-in-motion.

[3b (6) The tone-line
¶1 The synthesis of pitch, time, dynamic, and tensive relations, progressing into structural extent, constitutes the tone-line, i.e., the melodic/rhythmic/structural nucleus of pattern. [4a(4)]

14

[3 c. The *idioms* of pattern

¶1 The idioms of pattern are fundamental style concepts, deriving from characteristic associations of thematic, textural, and structural processes.

¶2 The range of idioms extends from the severest polyphony on the one hand, through a wide graduation of cross-idioms [3c(3)], to pure homophony on the other hand.

¶3 The opposite extremes of idiom, while not mutually exclusive, are based on somewhat contrary and restrictive premises.

[3c (1) Textural idioms

(a) Monolinear: texture*less* (successive thematic ideas)

1. Monophony

(b) Polylinear texture (simultaneous thematic ideas)

1. Polyphony: equivalent or competitive lines

a. Relation of the tone-lines in style

(1) Homogeneous

(2) Heterogeneous

b. Relations of the tone-lines in value. [4a(4d)]

(1) Equal value

(2) Unequal value

(3) Transfer of value from line to line

c. Relation of the tone-lines in register

(1) Same register

(2) Different registers

(3) Overlapping registers

2. Polyphony of the *stile famigliare* (homogeneous lines of melody in substantially unanimous rhythmic pattern—except for the possible indication of a *cantus firmus*—the whole texture forming progressing chords)

3. Polyphonically accompanied melody

4. Semi-polyphony (changing number and value of textural lines; "broken style") [3c(1d)]

5. Heterophony: dissociated simultaneous tone-lines

15

(c) Duolinear texture (successive thematic ideas; thematic melody and harmonic bass, expressed or implied, with intervening texture variable)

1. Homophony: disequal tone-lines

2. Semi-homophony (homophony with limited polyphonic detail) [3c(1)d]

3. Basso continuo homophony and semi-homophony (thematic melody and harmonic bass; texture improvised or supplied from partially definitive figurings associated with the bass) [4b(5a); 4b(7)¶2]

(d) Mixed textural idioms (intermixture of polylinear and duolinear characteristics of texture)[3c(1b)*4*; 3c(1c)*2*; cf.3c(3)]

[3c (2) Phraseological idioms (associated with textural idioms)

¶1 The primal structural processes of pattern lie in the *cursive* and *balanced* relations of the units of structure.

¶2 The following are the prevailing, though not rigid, distinctions between these idioms:

[3c(2) (a) Cursive phraseology, tends to be characteristic of polyphonic texture) [4c(2b)*1*]

1. A phenomenon of structural flow

2. Comprised of chains of units (indeterminate in number)

3. Asymmetrical

4. Open-ended

(b) Balanced phraseology (tends to be characteristic of homophonic texture) [4c(1b)*1*]

1. A phenomenon of structural pulse and counterpulse [4c(1b)*1*]

2. Comprised of pairs of units

3. Symmetrical

4. Potentially closed- or semiclosed-ended

(c) Mixed phraseology (intermixture of cursive and balanced phraseology)

[3c   (3) Cross-idioms

¶1 Middle styles result from the association of characteristics of linear and polylinear texture and phraseology in various mixtures.

¶2 Such hybrids have full individuality and validity in their own right, and offer their own special resources of pattern and expressive effect; e.g.,

    (a) Semi-polyphony [3c(1b)*4*]
    (b) Semi-homophony [3c(1c)*2*]

[3   d. The *aesthetic temperaments* underlying pattern

¶1 The basic aesthetic temperaments may be called "classic" and "romantic"; (Cf. "ethos" and "pathos").[7] In this connection, these terms do not refer to historical periods or movements.

¶2 The aesthetic temperaments are the index to the artistic ideal of the musical work and basic to its pattern and expressive effect.

(1) The classic and its inflections
    (a) The architectonic ideal
    (b) Formal abstract pattern
    (c) Objectivity
    (d) Impersonal mood
(2) The romantic and its inflections
    (a) The affective ideal
    (b) Individualistic, sometimes rhapsodic, pattern
    (c) Subjectivity
    (d) Idiosyncratic mood
(3) Eclecticism (mingling of classic and romantic traits in various proportions and emphases)

A. *Style from the Viewpoint of Pattern* (*continued*)

4. THE ELEMENTS OF PATTERN

¶1 The elements of pattern—its constituent factors—are integrated in living music under the compulsion of fundamental processes of progression. [5]

[7] See Curt Sachs, *The Commonwealth of Art,* New York, 1945, pp. 202ff.

¶2 The elements themselves, arbitrarily detached for observation, are here considered to be—

A. *Melody*/rhythm

B. *Texture*/rhythm (including melody and harmony, except in monophony which is textureless)

C. *Structure*/rhythm (including melody and texture)
¶3 The pervasive factor of *rhythm* [3b(2d)] is inherent in, and completely identified with, each and all of these elements, and cannot logically be set up as a separate element of the same order. One must therefore reject as illogical the cliché that "melody, rhythm, and harmony" constitute the "elements" of music. Rhythm can be considered separately only by assuming it as a point of view for observing a phase common to and a part of all of the elements. This special position of rhythm arises simply from the fact that music itself is a phenomenon of motion and time. [5a(1-2)]
¶4 In the relations among the elements, *melody*/rhythm stands preëminent. [4a] It is a part of texture and markedly conditions its progression. Both melody and texture are in turn embedded in structure, the progression of which melody largely motivates. [4b(8); 4c(1f)]
¶5 The concept of *texture*/rhythm, as considered here, embraces *melody*/rhythm [4b], while the aggregate of its tone-lines [4a(4b-d)] may also reveal in cross-section a composite of simultaneous and successive relations, which constitutes the specialized factor of *harmony*/rhythm. [4b(7)] The textural combination of tone-lines, however, may not always produce harmony in the above sense.
¶6 Melodic/rhythmic/textural progression is not conceivable without concomitant *structure*/rhythm. [4c]
¶7 For the inflective contribution of *dynamics,* see [3b(3c); 5a(1b)]. For the characterizing value of *tone color,* see [3a(5c); 3b(5)]

[4 a. *Melody*/rhythm/dynamics/structure/extent
¶1 The complex of melodic pattern, abbreviated in the topic above, is characterized by the interdependent actions of pitch change and rhythmic progression; at the same time, melodic

pattern embodies interpretative dynamic graduation and the progression of local structure into extent. [5c(9)]

¶2 The complex of melodic pattern is linear.

¶3 The basic or skeletal line of melody may sometimes be embedded in an elaborated texture, from which it must be extracted or inferred.

¶4 Even advancing harmonic masses have a melodic aspect. [4b(7)¶1]

[4a (1) Pitch pattern in melody
    (a) Basis of reference: the tone of reference
    (b) Range: Wide ... Narrow
    (c) Register
       1. Position within the unorientated gamut [3b(1a) *3*¶1] : High ... Low
       2. Position within the range of the instrument or voice: High register ... Low register
    (d) Contour (aural)
       1. Interval motion
         a. Repetitive
         b. Sinuous (degreewise)
         c. Angular (skipwise)
         d. Harmonic (cf. arpeggiate contour)
         e. Mixed: Simple ... Complicated
       2. Direction
         a. Ascending
         b. Descending
       3. Curvature
         a. Range of curve: Wide ... Narrow
         b. Peaks and dips
           (1) Relations among the peaks and dips
           (2) Mean level
           (3) Return curve (compensating)
           (4) Convolutions
             (a) Number
             (b) Complication
       4. Graphic shape (e.g., Bach's "wedge" fugue subject)

5. Artificially devised pitch pattern (e.g., B-A-C-H, A-S-C-H, etc.)

6. Pitch pattern produced by methods of chance [28a(4)vLG¶1]

[4a(1) (e) Relation to mode

1. Diatonic (employing tones belonging to the mode)

2. Chromatic (employing one tone or more foreign to the mode)

(f) Configuration

1. Essential line

2. Decorated line (melismatic, florid, ornamented, figurated, coloratura)

3. Mixed

(g) Tensity

1. Interval relations

¶1 Successive interval relations in the tone-line impart a shade of organic color to melody. [3b(4a)]

a. Consonance (detense)
(1) Perfect consonance
(2) Imperfect consonance
b. Dissonance (intense)
(1) Soft dissonance
(2) Hard dissonance

2. Tendency

a. Intense-detense activity in the pitch contour
b. Leaning characteristics of tones (dissonant, chromatic)
c. Momentum (sequential, scalar) [5c(6e)]

[4a (2) Rhythmic pattern in melody

(a) Basis of reference: the accented beat

(b) Accentuation

1. Rising accentuation (approach to point of emphasis; anacrusis, up-beat)

2. Falling accentuation (recession from point of emphasis; lag; cf. the feminine ending)

(c) Relation of the pattern to the beat

1. Coincidence of the tones of the pattern with the beats

2. Partial disagreement of the tones of the pattern with the beats

3. Subdivision of the beat by the pattern: Marked ... Limited

4. Grouping of the beats by the pattern; see (d) below.

(d) Relation of the pattern to the beat-group (in meter or measure)

1. Coincidence (with falling accentuation)

2. Disagreement (with rising accentuation)

3. Temporary change of the beat-grouping occasioned by the pattern of the tone-group (changing diaeresis; e.g., hemiola)

4. Disagreement of the pattern accent with the beat-group accent: syncopation (temporary eclipse of the group-accent, in favor of a preceding or succeeding rhetorical or agogic accent)

(e) Rhythmic activity: Marked ... Slight, Intermittent

(f) Rhythmic variety: Marked ... Slight, Irregular

(g) Rhythmic tensity

1. Intensive-detensive activity in the rhythmic pattern

2. Rhythmic momentum

(h) Outside influences on rhythmic pattern

1. Language patterns

2. Dance patterns

3. Delineative or descriptive patterns [6b(1c)]

[4a (3) Dynamic pattern in melody

(a) Basis of reference: mean level of sound intensity

[4a(3) (b) Tensity
  1. Basic level
    a. Even level maintained
    b. Fluctuation: Wide . . . Limited
  2. Compound levels (level within level)
  (c) Rate of dynamic change: Immediate (dynamic accent, sforzando) . . . Gradual, Varied

[4a (4) Synthesis of pitch, rhythmic, and dynamic patterns in melodic pattern
  (a) Basis of reference: an association of pitch and time points of reference
  (b) The tone-line (motion in pitch, time, and dynamics, interacting in one comprehensive, continuing, linear pattern)
  (c) Balance of ingredients
    1. Different emphases among the ingredients
    2. Such emphases are the basis of the individualization of the tone-line.
  (d) Value distinctions in the tone-line
    1. Thematic idea (capable of exercising a function in structure)
    2. Companion idea (differentiated co-equal)
    3. Attending idea, sometimes decorated (e.g., obbligato melody)
    4. Ancillary idea (of less distinctive value)
    5. Subordinate tone-line (non-distinctive)
    6. Intermittent filler (e.g., in semi-polyphony or semi-homophony) [3c(1b)4; 3c(1c)2]
    7. Harmonic bass-like tone-line
    8. Stationary tone-line (i.e., pedalpoint)
    9. Declamatory idea (associated chiefly with language)
  ¶1 Important types: plain chant, Monteverdi, Lully, Purcell, Bach, Mozart, Wagner-Strauss, Debussy, Schönberg (*Sprechstimme*)

[4a(4) (e) Phraseological idiom [3c(2)]
    1. Cursive (chain)
    2. Balanced (pair)
    3. Mixed

  (f) Span length
    1. Short (frequent cadences)
    2. Long (less frequent or concealed cadences)

  (g) Span junction
    1. Conjunct
    2. Disjunct

  (h) Span accentuation
    1. Regular (2, 4, 8, etc. accent pulse)
    2. Irregular (3, 5, 7, etc. accent pulse)

  (j) Contingency of melodic style on—
    1. Medium
    2. Idiom
    3. Aesthetic temperament
    4. Nationality

  (k) Influences affecting melody
    1. Language
    2. Folk *melody*/rhythm

[4a(4) (m) Melodic progression
    ¶1 The interests of melodic progression are largely identical with, contributory to, and contained within, those of structural progression. [4c(1f)]

    1. Melodic progression enters into all of the processes of progression as a primary factor and shares the impulses to progression in these processes.

    2. The impulses to progression more narrowly specific to melody
      a. The impulse of the intensive-detensive relations in the pitch contour
      b. The impulse of the pitch-contouring process to achieve valid shape as idea [4a(5)]

23

c. The impulse of the pulsing and measuring activity of the rhythmic pattern

d. The integrative impulse of the melodic pattern (as a whole) [5c(6a-h)]

[4a   (5) Melody as idea

(a) Melody of thematic quality transcends mere patterned value.

(b) Melody is a concept in the field of pitch-time-dynamics and possesses idea-quality.

(c) Melody is a logical projection of musical thought, in pattern and expressive effect.

(d) Melody of thematic quality is strongly distinguished by functional behavior. [5c(2)]

(e) Melody of thematic quality is distinguished by individuality of style.

(g) Melody of thematic quality is an indefinable flash of artistic insight.

(h) Melody epitomizes the nature of the composition of which it is the nucleus.

[4 b. *Texture* (including harmony)/melody/rhythm/dynamics/structure

¶1 The complex of textural pattern, abbreviated in the topic above, is characterized by simultaneous, cross-linear, and successive motion; at the same time textural pattern embodies dynamic differentiation among the lines, dynamic graduation, harmonic progression (especially positive in homophony), and projection of the local structure by interlinear thematic distribution (chiefly in polyphony and semi-polyphony.)
¶2 The complex of textural pattern is linear, polylinear, and interlinear.

(1) Textural distribution

(a) Number of lines: Constant ... Variable

(b) Spacement of lines: Close ... Spread

(2) Textural mass (the aggregate of the lines): Constant ... Variable

24

(3) Interlinear relations of texture
   (a) Motion between and among the lines
     1. Parallel
     2. Contrary
     3. Oblique
     4. Mixed

[4b(3) (b) Textural rhythm (the progressing composite rhythmic pattern of all the lines): Uniform . . . Varied

[4b   (4) Interlinear textural perspective
    (a) Depth of texture: Foreground activity . . . Background activity
    (b) Relative value of the lines [4a(4d)]
      1. Basis of value
        a. Thematic definition
        b. Rhythmic activity
      2. Balance among the lines: Equal . . . Unequal, Changing
    (c) Distinctions among the lines
      1. Style relation
        a. Identical
        b. Homogeneous
        c. Heterogeneous
      2. Dynamic relations: Equal . . . Unequal, Changing [15d(3e)]
      3. Timbre relations (instrumental, vocal)
        1. Identical
        2. Similar
        3. Different
    (d) Textural balance
      1. Constant
      2. Changing
    (e) Multiple texture (two or more distinguishable, simultaneous textures, e.g., polyphonically accompanied duo)

(5) Implied texture

(a) *Basso continuo* texture (leaves to the performer the actual realization of the texture, sometimes with the guidance of partially definitive figurings) [3c(1c) *3*; 4b(7)¶2]

(b) Outlined texture

1. Arpeggiated chords or incomplete chords may take the place and assume the function of chord masses.

2. Unnotated continuations of tones may be implied and imagined, or held as diminishing sounds, as, for example, with the sustaining pedal of the piano or on the harp.

[4b (6) Textural decoration

(a) Florid scale elaborations of the texture

(b) Florid arpeggiated elaborations of the texture

(c) Rapid oscillations between tones as elaboration of the texture

(7) The harmonic aspect of texture

¶1 Harmony is a succession of cross-sections of the lines of texture, moving as an advancing tone mass, and basically motivated by melody.

¶2 Note that some tones of the tone mass may be absent from a given cross-section, but are implied. [3c(1c)*3*; 4b(5)]

¶3 Observe that the harmonic factors set forth in [4b(7-8)] constitute in effect a system of *harmonic analysis*.

(a) The chord as an organism (a *systematic* combination of intervals and an organic color sonority)

1. The chord unit: conventionally considered as systematically "erected on a generating root," to form a triad, tetrad, pentad, etc., using tones from within the prevailing tone system (e.g., major, minor, Dorian, whole-tone, duodecuple, etc.) [3b (1b)]

¶1 A chord so formed, when erected as far as possible, returns to an octave of its root.

[4b(7a) *2.* Chord formation

> *a.* A chord is systematically erected in any tone system, on any root, by using as the interval of erection a 3rd, 4th, or 5th, or by alternating two of them; see *b* below.

¶1 Tones from *within* the prevailing tone system are *diatonic* by definition, and a melody or chord formed from them is diatonic. [4a(1e)*1*; 4b(7b)*1a(2a)*]

¶2 Tones may also be introduced from *outside* the prevailing tone system, in place of or in addition to one or more of the diatonic tones. Such tones are *chromatic,* and a melody or chord containing one or more of them is chromatic. [4a(1c)*2*; 4b(7b) *1a(2b)*]

¶3 The idea of the chromatic disappears in the 12-tone gamut [3b(1b)*3b-c*], unless micro-tones are introduced. [3b(1b)*4*] The concept of "all chromatic" is a contradiction.

> *b.* Interval systems of chord formation

¶1 The tones of a systematically erected chord may be arranged in any order (i.e., inversion or position.) In chords erected in perfect 4ths or 5ths the effect of inversion is likely to be obscured or eliminated.

> > *(1)* System of 3rds (maj., min., aug., dim.): erected on any root to form a 3-tone chord (triad), 4-tone chord (7th), 5-tone chord (9th), 6-tone chord (11th), 7-tone chord (13th)
> >
> > *(2)* System of 5ths (perfect): erected on any root to form a 3-tone chord (triad), etc. through a 7-tone chord

¶1 Not free from the system of 3rds

> > *(3)* System of 4ths (perfect): erected on any root to form a 3-tone chord (triad), etc. through a 7-tone chord

[4b(7a)*2* > *c.* A chord formation may be erected on any root from the tones of a series or tonerow [3b(1b)*3c*]
>
> *d.* Any chord formation, on any root, by any interval, may be erected from the tones of the 12-tone gamut. [3b(1b)*3b-c*]

e. Chords may be conceived as formed from mixtures of interval systems.

f. Polychordal combinations may be formed from two or more different chord formations; (single combinations or in polyharmonic progression).

g. A tone or tones may be added as a color fringe to any chord.

3. Textural spacement or distribution of the component tones of a chord: Close . . . Open

4. The non-chordal color mass (unsystematic; cf. the tone cluster) [4b(7c)*1*]

[4b(7) (b) Harmonic progression

    1. Tensity

      a. Intense

        (1) Harmony a positive, functional participant in progression

        (2) Tonal orientation (hierarchal)

          (a) Diatonic chords: tonal functions

            1' Primary: T D S$_D$

            2' Substitute primary (various combinations of tones over a primary bass root)

            3' Secondary: S$_T$ M S$_M$

          (b) Chromatic chords (chords with one tone or more foreign to the prevailing mode or scale)

            1' Chromatic substitutes for the diatonic tonal functions

              a' Functions maintained (largely referable to concentric tonalities) [3b(1b)*2b*]

              b' Functions obscured

            2' Chromatic chords, passive or lacking in function, *attendant to* and dependent on the diatonic functions, or on other chromatic chords with function

(c) Characteristics diatonic root bass progressions (in order of stylistic preference); cf. [4b(7b)*1b(2c)*]

1' 5th up or down

2' 4th up or down

3' 3rd down (less often up)

4' 2nd up or down

(d) A degree of incompatibility exists between the intense, strongly controlled, functional activity of tonal progression, and the melodic independence of polylinear styles, e.g., in the bass; cf. [4b(7b)*1b(2c)*]

b. Detense

(1) Harmony a passive, largely unfunctional participant in progression

[4b(7b)*1b*]   *(2)* Modal orientation (largely non-hierarchal)

(a) Diatonic chords (limited modal functions)

1' Tonal T (limited largely to local influence)

2' Modal D (chiefly in cadences)

3' Other chords form a largely functionless pool of chords of the mode

(b) Chromatic chords (selective chromatic substitutions for diatonic chords of the mode)

(c) Characteristic diatonic root bass progressions (in order of stylistic preference; motivated by melodic style; cf. [4b(7b)*1a (2c)*] and note the reverse order)

1' 2nd up or down

2' 3rd up or down

3' 4th up or down

4' 5th up or down

(*d*) A marked degree of compatibility exists between the detense, limitedly controlled functional activity of modal progression, and the melodic independence of polylinear styles, e.g., in the bass; cf. [4b(7b)*1a(2d)*]

[4b(7b)*1*] *c.* Supertense

(*1*) Harmony a non-functional succession of dissonances

(*2*) Amodal (atonal) progressions of varying degrees of intense dissonance

(*a*) Chords from the systems of 4ths and 5ths, melodically guided or in a flow of color

(*b*) Successions of harmonic combinations derived from a series or tonerow, progressing under tonerow melodic and color influence

(*c*) Non-chordal combinations resulting from dissonant polyphony

(*d*) Mixtures

(*e*) Complete compatibility exists between the supertense, functionally uncontrolled activity of amodal progression, and the melodic independence of polylinear styles.

[4b(7b)] *2.* Rate of progression (i.e., of chord change): Frequent . . . Infrequent

3. Basis of harmonic progression

a. Orientative choices of progression

b. Harmonic color choices of progression

c. Manipulation of the harmonic functions (importance of the succession of roots and behavior of the bass)

d. Correlation of progressions with local harmonic and structural rhythm

4. Harmonic momentum (orientative and rhythmic impulses) [5c(6e)]

5. Polyharmonic progression (two or more simultaneous streams of progression)

6. Chord-stream color (color of the successions of organic color)

    a. Diatonic

        (1) Detense color

        (2) Emphasis on relation

    b. Chromatic

        (2) Intense color

        (2) Emphasis on side-slip relation or on non-relation

    c. Mixtures

7. Overbloom of harmonic color added through the use of the sustaining pedal of the piano

[4b(7) (c) Non-chordal combinations in succession

    1. Arbitrary non-chordal combinations as organic color (e.g., the tone cluster)

    2. Polyphonically produced combinations passed through

(8) Textural progression

¶1 A complex of melodic/rhythmic and harmonic/rhythmic progressions

    (a) Melodic progression [4a(4m)]

    (b) Harmonic progression [4b(7b)]

[4b(8) (c) Voice leading in progression in—

    1. Homophony

    2. Polyphony

    3. Modality

    4. Tonality

    5. Behavior of the bass in—

        a. Homophony (primarily as a harmonic foundation)

        b. Polyphony (as a melodic ingredient, sometimes also as a harmonic foundation)

        c. Tonality [4b(7b)*1a(2c)*]

        d. Modality [4b(7b)*1b(2c)*]

(d) Melodic-harmonic progression in—

1. Consonant agreement of melody and harmony

2. Dissonant disagreement of melody and harmony (non-chord tones)

(e) Progression through the tensities of textural/harmonic progression

(f) Interlinear rhythmic progression (textural rhythm)

(g) Interlinear dynamic progression

(h) Progression through differentiations of mass

(j) Progression through fluctuating perspective (distribution of interest through changing value relations among the lines) [4b(4)]

(k) Progression through changing degrees of textural complexity

[4 c. *Structure*/thematic melody/rhythm/texture (including harmony)/dynamics/extent

¶1 The complex of structural pattern, abbreviated in the topic above, is characterized by the projection, either linearly or interlinearly, of the thematic ideas of local structure into extent [5c(9)]; at the same time, the melodic-structural progression is usually supported by coöperative harmonic progression (especially in homophony), and enhanced by dynamic inflection; the evolving structural concept brings into being the structural time in which the pattern progresses. [5c(9a)]

¶2 The complex of structural pattern is linear or polylinear. Linear structure comprises monophony and various manifestations of homophony; polylinear structure comprises more and less intense polyphony and semi-polyphony.

¶3 The units of motive, phrase, motive-as-phrase, and theme, constitute the basic substance of linear and polylinear structure. [4c(1a)*1*; 4c(2a)*1*] Motive as such may function as a generating factor of construction; or, motive may be contained within theme. Phrase or motive-as-phrase is contained within theme.

¶4 The motive is especially characteristic of polylinear structure, and the theme of linear structure. All of the larger structural entities, to the finally fulfilled design of a work, are expansions of these units, and are subject to the various processes of linear and polylinear organization.

¶5 Observe that the structural factors set forth in [4c] and [5c] constitute in effect a system of *form analysis.* Contributions to form analysis may be found also in other parts of the *Handbook,* since form is simply one aspect of style.

[4c   (1) *Linear* structure

    (a) Structural elements

        1. Units and spans of structure

            a. Motive (a germinal unit of idea value, indeterminate in length)

            b. Figure (a motive of sub-idea value, often in formal passage-work)

            c. Phrase (a member of an interdependent pair or group of units)

            d. Motive-as-phrase

            e. Period (a balanced pair or group of units or sections)

            f. Theme (an idea of sufficient value to motivate and support structural design) (for rhythmic theme, see serial rhythmic structure [4c(2h)*6*])

            g. Division

            h. The integral form [4c(1h)]

            j. The cycle of movements [4c(1j)]

        2. Demarkation of units by means of—

            a. Caesura, cadence[8]

            b. Pattern change

            c. Thematic change

            d. Mood change

            e. Style change

[8] See the author's ''View of the Cadence in Modern Contra-tonal Systems,'' in *Volume of Proceedings* of the Music Teachers' National Association, series 27, 1934, pp. 209-223.

[4c(1) (b) Structural idioms

        1. Balanced structure (characteristic of linear structure) [3c(2b)]

¶1 Balanced structure evolves under the influence of a hierarchy of spans. [4c(1d); 5c(3b)*2*]

¶2 Balanced structure is marked by—

        a. Sectional construction
        b. Relation of units in pair or pair of pairs
        c. Disjunct contact of spans
        d. Symmetrical, or simulated symmetrical, proportion through qualitatively intensive aesthetic length [5a(4c)]
        e. Potentially closed-ended structure
        f. Periodic or quasi-periodic expansion

        2. Cursive structure, as in [4c(2b)*1*] (less frequent in linear structure than in polylinear)

        3. Mixed structure

[4c(1) (c) Structural phraseology

¶1 The notion of "regularity" is based on the prevalence of alternation of emphasis in linear structure, with resultant symmetry. [4c(1d); 5c(4)]

        1. Inherent regularity (2+2, 2+2, etc.)

        2. Inherent irregularity (2+3; 3+2; 3+4; etc.)

        3. Incorporated irregularity

        a. Extension
        b. Interpolation
        c. Elision (structural overlap)
        d. Ellipsis
        e. Augmentation of the cadence rhythm

[4c(1) (d) Structural rhythm

¶1 Structural rhythm is the quality of structure resulting from the accretion of spans (phrases, etc.) by pulse and counterpulse.

        1. Simple accentuation among the spans

        a. Duple (i.e., stronger rhythmic emphasis on alternate spans) *b.* Triple (i.e., stronger rhythmic emphasis on every third span; less common than duple)

c. Spans may be disposed by rising or falling accentuation [4a(2b)]

2. Compound accentuation among the spans

a. Pairs or threes of spans within still larger spans

b. Super-accentuation (the larger spans themselves may be disposed by rising or falling accentuation)

3. Rhythmic hierarchy of spans under analogy [5c(3b)*2*; 5c(3d)*1*]

(e) Structural dynamics

1. Dynamic changes confirm and enhance all of the factors in the structural pattern, both local and extensive.

2. Dynamic scale

a. Simple contrast: Wide contrast . . . Limited contrast, Varied contrast

b. Compound contrast (dynamic level within level)

c. Contrasts between divisions and movements are contingent on the interests of the style.

3. Rate of dynamic change: Immediate . . . Gradual, Varied

4. The structural dynamic pattern and its effect are based on the manipulation of the range and rate of change.

[4c(1) (f) Structural progression

¶1 Melodic/rhythmic and textural/rhythmic progression are embedded in structural progression. [4a(4m); 4b(7b); 4b(8)]

¶2 Structural progression is the core of the larger progression of pattern, and is involved with and dependent on the processes of progression. [5c]

¶3 The contributions of the processes of progression to structural progression are as follows:

1. Orientation: supports structural progression through the pattern of changing cadential points of reference [5c(1)] : Wide cadence contrast . . . Limited cadence contrast

2. Thematic function: supports structural progression through the pattern of thematic behavior in shaping and individualizing the structure [5c(2)] : Strong support . . . Limited support

3. Analogy: supports structural progression through the pattern of assertion and counterassertion [5c(3)] : Compact analogies . . . Loose analogies, Few analogies

4. Proportion: supports structural progress through the pattern of comparative span lengths [5c(4)] : Regular, Irregular, Mixed

[4c(1f)   *5.* Contrast: supports structural progression through the pattern of opposing similarities and dissimilarities [5c(5)] : Marked contrast . . . Limited contrast, Immediate contrast . . . Evolving contrast

6. Integration: supports structural progression through the pattern of expanding logic [5c(6)] : Intense . . . Detense, Contra-integrative [5c(6j)]

7. Aesthetic pace: supports structural progression through the pattern of changing tensities [5c(7)] : Intense . . . Detense, Even, Fluctuating, Cumulative

8. Equilibrium: supports structural progression through the pattern of imbalances and compensations [5c(8)] : Marked compensation . . . Limited compensation

9. Extent: supports structural progression through the pattern of interacting quantitative and qualitative differences [5c(9)] : Marked difference . . . Limited difference

36

10. Mood distribution: supports structural progression through the pattern of mood change [5c(10)]: Wide mood contrast (Rapid change, dramatic . . . Slow change, evolving lyric; Varied change, lyrico-dramatic) . . . Limited mood contrast, lyric

11. Style distribution: supports structural progression through the pattern of style change [5c(11)]: Wide style contrast . . . Limited style contrast, Varied style contrast

4c(1) (g) Structural procedures; see [4c(2h)]

¶1 Some of the structural procedures of polylinear structure may occasionally be introduced in linear structure.

¶2 The device of thematic mutation, more especially associated with polylinear structure, may also be found in linear structure, with or without imitation; cf. [4c(2d)*4*]

4c(1) (h) Structural pattern of *integral linear* forms

¶1 Different employments of the structural elements, idioms, and structural progression, in characteristic patterns governed by practice and convention, produce certain recognized structural formulae—the "forms"; SEE TERMS, p. XI.

1. The integral forms (cf. integral with composite) [4c(1j)]

a. Unitary (period-form)

b. Multiple (stanza-form; *ostinato*-based form; homophonic chaconne, passacaglia; variation-form)

c. Additive (some elementary dance structures; some opera overtures)

d. Cursive chain (homophonic through-developed forms)

e. Cursive with reprise (monophonic and homophonic through-developed forms with short or partial terminal reprise)

f. Symmetrically balanced (binary-form; cf. below: *j.* Circular, *k.* Circular bowed)

37

g. Asymmetrically balanced (expanded binary-form; monophonic and homophonic Bar-form; monophonic ballade-form)

h. Alternating (rondo-form; monophonic rondeau-form; monophonic virelai-form)

j. Circular (ternary-form; sonata-form)

k. Circular bowed (bowed rondo-form; bowed sonata-form)

¶1 A bowed form (*Bogenform*) reverses the order of themes in reprise, e.g., AB C BA; cf. Retrograde. [4c(2h)*4*; 4c(2j)*1k*]

m. Hybrids (rondo-sonata-form, etc.)

n. Sui generis (fantasia-forms, unique forms)

[4c(1h) *2*. Formulation of the principle distinctive to each of the conventional forms; e.g.,

¶1 The principle of the expanded binary-form is that of maintenance of a quality of balance between a shorter initial division and an asymmetrically longer succeeding division, in a circular linear frame.

¶2 The principle of the sonata-form is that of projecting as counterfoils two antithetical or complementary themes (or groups), in a circular linear frame: first, in an incomplete and expectant exposition, in contrasting tonal or other orientations; then, in developmental exploitation with increased instability and tensity, and in changing orientations; finally, in compensating re-relation and reconsideration of the themes, in stable orientative and structural finality.

[4c(1h) *3*. Modification of *integral linear* forms

¶1 Forms may be inflected from the conventional norm by changed internal emphasis or rearrangement. Such individual views of the forms create fresh structural resources.

a. Changed proportion, toward asymmetry (expanded binary-form: e.g., Bach, Overture 2, D maj., II, Aria)

b. Changed aesthetic pace (intrinsic tensity altered, extent qualitatively modified)

38

(1) Intensified (condensed sonata-form: e.g., Beethoven, Sonata 32, C min., op. 111, I, pianoforte)

(2) Detensified

c. Changed aesthetic temperament (from the architectonic toward the affective)

(1) Toward the lyric (lyric sonata-form: e.g., Schubert, Symphony 8, B min., "Unfinished," I)

(2) Toward the dramatic (sonata-form, with representative themes and simultaneous reprise: e.g., Wagner, Overture to *Die Meistersinger*)

d. Changed style variety

(1) Increased (sectionalized sonata-form: e.g., Tchaikovsky, Symphony 6, B min., op. 74, I)

(2) Decreased

[4c(1)   e. Changed extent

(1) Expanded (expanded sonata-form: e.g., Beethoven, Symphony 9, D min., op. 125, I)

(2) Contracted

f. Changed fusion and continuity

(1) Increased (developed asymmetrical ternary-form: e.g., Wagner, Vorspiel to *Tristan und Isolde*)

(2) Decreased

g. Change of themes toward interrelation (thematically derivative sonata-form, bowed: e.g., Liszt, *Les Préludes*)

h. Change under the influence of medium (multiple-theme, double-exposition sonata-form: e.g., Beethoven, Concerto 4, G maj., op. 58, I, pianoforte)

j. Mingling of characteristics of different form-types (rondo-variation-sonata-form: e.g., Bee-

39

thoven, Symphony 9, D min., op. 125, III; sonata-
ternary-rondo-form: Schumann, Phantasie, C
maj., op. 17, I, pianoforte)

k. Change of form toward a different idiom
(homophonic and polyphonic interassociation, as
in a combination of fugal and rondo or sonata
characteristics: e.g., Mahler, Symphony 5, C♯
min., III-5, Rondo-Finale)

m. Change of form from the conventional norm
under the influence of text, title, or program [6b]
(fused and reversed variation-form: e.g., d'Indy,
Istar Variations, orchestra; through-developed
rondo-variation-sonata-form: e.g., R. Strauss,
Till Eulenspiegels lustige Streiche, F maj., op.
28; through-developed transformation-variation-
form: R. Strauss, *Don Quixote,* D maj., op. 35)

[4c(1)] (j) Structural pattern of *composite linear* forms

¶1 A cycle is a significantly associated group of movements,
and is based on and distinguished by the type, form, mood,
style, emphasis, and arrangement, of the separate movements;
the comprehensive pattern of a cycle is a reflection of a large-
scale manipulation of the structural tensities. [4c(3)] [9]

[4c(1j)] *1.* Cyclic forms (sometimes with incidental polyphonic interest)

a. Additive cycle (indeterminate number of contrasting movements; e.g., baroque ordre, sonata
da camera, suite; early classic divertimento,
serenade, cassation; romantic suite)

b. Alternating cycle (alternation of relative intensity and detensity)

(1) Cursive with conjunction: S-F (—S) (e.g.,
French Overture); S-F S-F (e.g., some baroque sonatas, concerti grossi)

(2) Cursive expanded: S-F S F S(or M) F,

---

[9] See Lucile Umbreit, *The Evolution of the Cyclic Idea from the 16th Century
to the High Classic Period,* thesis for the A.M. degree, Vassar College, 1936.

and others (e.g., some baroque sonatas, concerti grossi)

c. Tapering cycle (from relative intensity to relative detensity)

(1) Circular: F S F (e.g., Italian overture; early classic symphony, quartet, sonata; classic concerto, sonata; classic and romantic concerto)

(2) Circular expanded: F S M F (e.g., classic and romantic symphony, quartet, sonata)

d. Cumulative cycle (sustainment of different shades of intensity)

¶1 The order of the S and M movements may sometimes be reversed; and the M movement may be supplanted by a type of F movement, as in the Scherzo.

(1) Sustained: F S M F (e.g., classic and romantic symphony, concerto, quartet, sonata)

(2) Sustained expanded (enlarged movements, sometimes additional movements): F S M F (e.g., late classic and romantic symphony, quartet, sonata)

e. Equalized cycle (approximately equal shades of tensity) (e.g., Honegger, Symphony 2, D, 1941)

f. Discursive cycle (dispersion of different shades of tensity, usually governed by a program) (e.g., Berlioz, *Harold en Italie*, G maj., op. 16)

[4c(1j)] *2.* Modification of cyclic forms

¶1 Cycles may be changed from the conventional norm by thematic interrelation of the movements, or by extra-musical influence.

a. Cycle with thematic allusions (e.g., Beethoven, Symphony 5, C min., op. 67)

b. Cycle with community of themes (e.g., symphony:

César Franck, Symphony, D min.; suite: Rimsky-Korsakoff, *Scheherazade,* E min.-maj., op. 35)

c. Continuous cycle (in integral circular or other linear frame; e.g., Bartók, Quartet 3 for strings: part I, part II, part III—recapitulation of part I, part IV—coda)

d. Fused cycle (continuous and with community of themes) (e.g., concerto: Liszt, Concerto, E♭ maj., pianoforte; symphony: Sibelius, Symphony 7, C maj., op. 105)

e. Cycle changed from the conventional norm under the influence of title or program (e.g., program symphony: Liszt, Faust Symphony, C maj.-min.; program suite: Rimsky-Korsakoff, *Scheherazade,* C min.-maj., op. 35)

[4c   (2) *Polylinear* structure (in a linear frame) [4c(2e)]
(a) Structural elements; cf. [4c(1a)]
    1. Units and spans of structure
      a. Motive
      b. Figure
      c. Phrase (tends to be used cursively in polylinear structure)
      d. Motive-as-phrase
      e. Period (less frequent in polylinear structure than in linear)
      f. Theme (for rhythmic theme, see serial rhythmic structure [4c(2h)*6*])
      g. Division (often conjunct)
      h. The integral form [4c(2j)]
      j. The cycle of movements [4c(2k)]
    2. Demarcation of units by means of—
      a. Caesura, cadence
        (1) In the individual line (without coincidences with cadences in other lines; staggered cadences)

(2) In the aggregate of lines (coincidence of cadences in the majority or all of the lines)

b. Pattern change

c. Thematic change

d. Mood change

e. Style change

[4c(2)   (b) Structural idioms

1. Cursive structure (characteristic of polylinear structure) [3c(2a)]

¶1 Cursive structure is marked by—

a. Continuous construction

b. Relation of units in chain or evolving succession

c. Indeterminate number of spans

d. Conjunct or covered contact of spans

e. Asymmetrical proportion

f. Potentially open-ended structure

g. Relevant continuation or through-developed expansion

2. Balanced structure, as in [4a(1b)*1*] less frequent in polylinear structure than in linear)

3. Mixed structure

[4c(2)   (c) Textural interlinear relations

1. Interlinear distribution of melodic values

a. Homogeneous lines

b. Heterogeneous lines

c. Equal lines

d. Unequal lines

e. Polyphonically accompanied melody

f. Semi-polyphony

2. Interlinear differentiation based on distinctions of—

a. Melodic pitch contour

b. Rhythmic pattern

c. Cadence location (cadences staggered among the lines)

d. Phraseological pattern

e. Dynamic pattern

f. Climax pattern

g. Melodic value

[4c(2) (d) Structural interlinear processes

¶1 The structural interlinear processes are also essentially structural procedures. [4c(2h)]

1. Thematic exchange (*Stimmtausch*) (related to imitation; when continued, produces a form, e.g., the rondellus-form)

2. Thematic imitation

a. Successive imitation

(*1*) Essential (cf. the fugue)

(*2*) Incidental (such imitation is sometimes approximate)

b. Overlapping imitation

(*1*) Canonic (when continued, produces the canon-form, which carries along concurrently the form of the imitated melody)

(*2*) Canonic exposition (e.g., in the ricercar, etc.)

(*3*) Stretto (e.g., in the fugue-form, etc.)

c. Fugal exposition (when continued, produces the fugue-form)

d. Approximate imitation (i.e., thematic antiphony; successive or overlapping)

3. Motive or phrase imitation, exact or approximate (as distinguished from thematic imitation, exact or approximate)

4. Thematic mutation, with or without imitation

¶1 The device of thematic mutation may also occur incidentally in linear structure, with or without imitation. [4c(lg)¶2]

(*a*) Augmentation

(*b*) Diminution

(*c*) Inversion

(*d*) Retrograde (continuation of the original by its retrograde produces the integral palindrome-form) [4c(2h)*4*]

(*e*) Combinations of *(a)* with *(c)* or *(d);* or *(b)* with *(c)* or *(d)*; etc.

[4c(2)   (e) The linear frame of interlinear activity

¶1 The focus of most polyphonic styles is prevailingly on their interlinear activities. These activities nevertheless take place in structural time and hence fall within a linear frame. The inherent intensity of interlinear activity—the content of the structural divisions—tends to overshadow the linear pattern which orders these divisions. The relations of the divisions are likely to differ from those of purely linear structure, and the extensive structural progression is accordingly qualified.

1. Structural divisions

a. Conjunction through dove-tailed cadences (between lesser divisions)

(*1*) In some lines

(*2*) In all lines

b. Disjunction through simultaneous cadences in all lines (between greater divisions)

(*1*) With style continued

(*2*) With style contrasted

c. Momentary rhetorical disjunction

2. Imbalance among divisions

a. Unequal length

b. Unequal tensity

[4c(2e)   *3.* Relation of divisions

a. Homogeneous thematic material (e.g., the ricercar on one theme)

b. Contrasted thematic material (e.g., the canzona; the ricercar on more than one theme;

double, triple, etc., fugue with successive expositions)

c. Inclination to less modal or tonal contrast than in linear structure

d. Inclination to less style contrast than in linear structure

e. Inclination to continuity, covering the points of division

[4c(2)   (f) Structural dynamics

    1. As in [4c(1e)*1*]

    2. As in [4c(1e)*2*]; also:

    a. Dynamic scale is likely to be more limited in polylinear structure than in linear structure.

    3. Rate of dynamic change

    a. Dynamic change usually cannot take place as rapidly in polylinear structure as in linear structure.

4. In polylinear structure, the separate lines are inflected by dynamic changes characteristic of each line and not necessarily correspondent among the lines.

[4c(2)   (g) Structural progression

¶1 As in [4c(1f)¶1]

¶2 As in [4c(1f)¶2]

¶3 With some exceptions the processes of progression contribute to polylinear structure in ways similar to those of linear structure. The correspondences are assumed and are indicated below only by the general references to [4c(1f)]; the exceptions, stated in comparison with parallel linear processes, are as follows:

    1. Orientation [4c(1f)*1*]

    a. Cadential contrast tends to be more limited.

    b. Modulatory contrast tends to be more limited.

    2. Thematic function [4c(1f)*2*]

    a. Thematic contrast tends to be more limited.

46

b. Hierarchal relations among themes tend to be less pronounced.

c. Thematic function is manifested linearly, in the linear frame of the polylinear structure.

d. Specialization of the thematic functions in polylinear structure [5c(2a)]

    (1) Exposition is characterized by imitation.

    (2) Exposition exactly restated in reprise is foreign to polylinear structure.

    (3) Exposition reformulated usually employs the interlinear processes [4c(2d)] and the effect of reprise is minimized.

    (4) The variant in polyphonic structure may take the form of alteration of the context rather than of the theme.

    (5) Development takes place through exploitation of the interlinear processes [4c(2d)], coupled with modulation.

[4c(2g)]   *3.* Analogy [4c(1f)*3*]

    a. Analogical relations in polylinear structure occur for the most part interlinearly in their own special terms. [5c(3c)*1b*]

4. Proportion [4c(1f)*4*]

    a. Proportional relations occur linearly (locally within each line and extensively within the linear frame of the structure).

    b. Proportions in polylinear structure tend to be asymmetrical, which reduces the interplay between regular and irregular structural spans.

5. Contrast [4c(1f*5*]

    a. Contrast tends to be more limited, and to be evolving in character.

6. Integration [4c(1f)*6*]

    a. Integration combines polylinear and linear forms of logical progression.

b. Structural progression tends to be intense.

c. Contra-integration scarcely exists [5c(6j)], except in logically inept polyphony.

[4c(2g)   *7.* Aesthetic pace [4c(1f)*7*]

a. The changing tensity of aesthetic pace occurs linearly within each line and interlinearly in the progression of the texture. [5c(7c)*2b*]

b. Intensity from competitive activity in the interlinear structure predominates.

c. Structural climax in polylinear structure tends to occur through interlinear involvements and progression toward complexity; this is an organic form of climax.

8. Equilibrium [4c(1f)*8*]

a. Polylinear structure, tending to be inherently asymmetrical, engages in less added imbalance and hence is less subject to the compensatory intervention of equilibrium.

9. Extent [4c(1f)*9*]

a. Polylinear structure, because of its preoccupation with local interlinear processes, is less intent on the projection of the linear aspect of structure; it is hence less strongly anticipative in fulfillment of the whole extent.

10. Mood distribution [4c(1f)*10*]

a. Change of mood tends to be less frequent and mood contrast more limited in polylinear progression.

11. Style distribution [4c(1f)*11*]

a. Change of style tends to be less frequent and style contrast more limited in polylinear progression.

[4c(2)   (h) Structural procedures

¶1 A structural procedure is a process incorporated in and conditioning the character of a structure, while not constituting the integral form itself.

48

¶2 The structural interlinear processes are akin to structural procedures [4c(2d)], but govern the structure locally rather than extensively.

[4c(2h)]¶3 While the procedures and structural interlinear processes tend to be native to polylinear structure, some of them may also sometimes be introduced into linear structure. [4c(1g)]

1. *Cantus firmus*-based structure

¶1 The form of the *cantus firmus* itself may be reflected in the integral form, which is frequently cursive.

2. *Ostinato*-based structure

¶1 The *ostinato* may underlie cursive, variation, and other integral forms.

3. Serial or tonerow-based structure

¶1 The tonerow or series, in simplest usage, is a sophisticated ostinato phenomenon, veiled by dispersal over the texture, indifferent to register and continuation in the same tone-line, and forming the basis of elaborative, often cursive structure. The tonerow is subject to inversion, retrograde, and retrograde inversion, to transposition and segmentation. Transposition of the tonerow is analogous to modulation; cf. [5c,1a)*6a(3)*]

4. Retrograde-based structure

¶4 The retrograde principle, by continuing the original with its retrograde, may be applied as a procedure, or may produce the integral palindrome-form [4c(2j)*1k*] ; (e.g., Schönberg, *Pierrot Lunaire*, op. 21, no. 18, Mondfleck)

5. Isorhythmic structure

¶1 Isorhythm is the repeated application of the same rhythmic pattern to successive portions of a continuing melody.

6. Serial rhythmic structure

¶1 The serial application of a rhythmic pattern may occur with or without association with the same pitch pattern.

¶2 Serial rhythmic structure may employ augmentation, diminution, or retrograde.

¶3 Cf. serial or tonerow-based structure. [4c(2h)*3*]

49

¶4 Cf. isorhythmic structure (essentially a form of rhythmic serialism). [4c(2h)5]

[4c(2)] (j) Structural pattern of *integral polylinear* forms
¶1 As in [4c(1h)¶1]

1. The integral forms; cf. integral with composite [4c(2k)]

a. Unitary (canon-form)

b. Multiple (ostinato-based form; polyphonic chaconne, passacaglia; polyphonic variations)

c. Additive (sectional canzona)

d. Cursive chain (*cantus firmus*-based form; through-developed cursive-form; fuga-form with several themes, as in the ricercar with several themes; continuous canzona-form; continuous tonerow-based form)

e. Cursive chain with reversions (cursive-form; fuga-form with one theme, as in the ricercar-form with one theme; some simple fugue-forms; double, triple, etc., fugue-forms with successive expositions)

f. Symmetrically balanced (semi-polyphonic binary-form; cf. *k.* Retrograde below)

g. Asymmetrically balanced (expanded semi-polyphonic binary-form; some fugue-forms)

h. Alternating (polyphonic rondeau, virelai, ballata)

j. Circular (some fugue-forms)

k. Retrograde (palindrome-form) [4c(2h)4]

m. Sui generis (fantasia-forms, unique forms)

[4c(2j)] 2. Formulation of the principle distinctive to each of the conventional forms; e.g.,

¶1 The principle of the fuga-form is that of successive canonic expositions of one or several themes, in a cursive linear frame.

¶2 The principle of the simple fugue-form is that of a succession of polyphonic expositions and re-expositions of an essential theme in imitative, responsorial statement and re-statement (subject-answer), in a bi-, tri-, or multi-partite linear frame: first, in expository presentation; then in successive re-expositions, in a chain of tonal or other orientations, the treatments being progressively diversified, given episodical relief, and brought cumulatively to stable completion.

¶3 One viewpoint considers the fugue to be a "procedure," not a "form," on the ground that its *linear* structure is indeterminate (bi-, tri-, or multi-partite.) This position minimizes the fact that polyphonic structure is, at the same time and perhaps more significantly, *polylinear*. In fact, the exploitation of the polylinear processes may be said to be the determinant of the variable linear frame. [4c(2e)] The linear aspect of polylinear structure is also to a considerable degree covered over by the inherent non-sectionality, overlapping, and continuity, of the polylinear processes.

[4c(2j)]   *3*. Modification of *integral polylinear* forms
¶1 As in [4c(1h)*3*¶1]

a. Changed aesthetic pace (intrinsic tensity altered, extent qualitatively modified)
(1) Intensified
(2) Detensified (e.g., loosely constructed fugues)

b. Changed extent
(1) Increased (fugue-form: e.g., Beethoven, Grosse Fuge, B♭, op. 133, string quartet)
(2) Decreased

c. Changed aesthetic temperament (from the formal toward the affective) (fugue-form: e.g., Liszt, Fantasie und Fuge on the Chorale in *Le Prophète,* organ)

d. Changed style variety
(1) Increased (e.g., the dramatically varied madrigals of Gesualdo)
(2) Decreased

e. Changed fusion and continuity

(1) Increased

(2) Decreased (fugue-form: e.g., Bach, Fugue from Toccata and Fugue, D min., organ, col. works, vol. 15, pp. 267-275)

f. Changes of type of thematic material (fugue-form: cf. Bach, Reger, and Hindemith fugues)

g. Change under the influence of medium (fugue-form: e.g., Beethoven, String Quartet, C♯ min., op. 131, I; Reger, Fugue from Variations and Fugue on a Theme by Mozart, op. 137, orchestra)

h. Mingling of characteristics of different forms (ricercar-fugue: e.g., Bach, Ricercar a 6 from *Das musikalische Opfer*)

j. Change under the influence of text, title, or program (fugue-form: e.g., R. Strauss, Finale (double fugue) from Sinfonia Domestica, op. 53)

[4c(2)(k) Structural pattern of *composite polylinear* forms

¶1 As in [4c(1j)¶1; 4c(3)]

¶2 The cycle in polylinear structure is somewhat less common and less highly developed than in linear structure.

1. Cyclic forms (with occasional mingling of semi-polyphony)

a. Embryonic cycle (e.g., sectional canzona in markedly contrasting divisions)

b. Pair of disparate movements (e.g., prelude and fugue)

c. Additive cycle (indeterminate number of contrasting movements) (e.g., baroque sonata da chiesa, polyphonic or semi-polyphonic suite)

[4c(2k)*1*   *d.* Alternating cycle (alternation of relative intensity and detensity)

(1) Cursive: S F̄ S F (e.g., baroque sonata da chiesa, concerto grosso)̄

(2) Cursive with conjunction: S-F̄ S-F̄ (e.g., baroque sonata da chiesa, concerto grosso)̄; F̄ S̄-F (e.g., Bach,

Toccata, Adagio, transition leading to Fugue, C maj.,
organ, col. works, vol. 15, pp. 262-266)
(3) Cursive expanded: S F̄ S F S(or M) F, and others
(e.g., some baroque sonatas, concerti grossi)

      e. Tapering cycle (from relative intensity to rel-
      ative detensity)

          (1) Circular: F̄ S F (e.g., semi-polyphonic
          sonata, concerto̅)

      f. Cycle within cycle (e.g., Bach, Das musikalische
      Opfer, Trio-sonata)

    2. Modification of cyclic forms

¶1 Polylinear cyclic forms are diverse rather than standard-
ized, and cases that might be considered as modifications of a
type are few. An instance might be found in the Prelude
and Fugue related thematically.

[4c   (3) *The cyclic principle* [4c (1j)¶1]

¶1 The basis of the cycle lies in the necessity for successive
rebeginnings in order to secure greater valid extent and its
attendant variety. [5c(9g)] The cyclic pattern is larger than
that of the integral form, but correspondingly less highly
organic, despite the contributions to a larger unity noted
under (b) below. Cyclic structure involves the following:

(a) Cyclic contrast among movements by means of
differences in—

    1. Thematic material
    2. Tonal or other orientation
    3. Tempo
    4. Meter or measure
    5. Internal movement structure
    6. Complexity
    7. Mood
    8. Style

(b) Cyclic unity among movements by means of—

    1. Community of motives or themes
    2. Tonal or other orientation
    3. Cyclic Continuity

4. Mood relation

5. Style relation

[4c(3)   (c) Cyclic progression by means of a comprehensive pattern of—

1. Cyclic orientation
2. Cyclic thematic material
3. Cyclic proportion
4. Cyclic contrast
5. Cyclic aesthetic pace
6. Cyclic tensity
7. Cyclic dynamics
8. Cyclic climax
9. Cyclic mood
10. Cyclic style

(d) Cyclic characterization

1. Cyclic characterization is determined by the differentiation of the movements in weight.

2. Greater relative weight of a movement is based on a combination of—

a. Relatively greater intensity of the pattern

b. Relatively greater complexity of the pattern

c. Relatively more intense sustainment of the logic

d. Relatively greater seriousness of the mood

e. Relatively greater scope of the extent

[4c   (4) *Superstructure*

¶1 Refers to the overall structure of an extensive work in numerous parts, such as an opera, music drama, ballet, or choral work.

(a) The more extensive and multipartite a structure is, the less it can be expected to conform specifically and in its particulars to the principles of integral and cyclic form.

(b) But, even though these principles may exert a more general and less categorical authority in superstructure than in integral and cyclic structure, their contribution to a superstructure in certain works is intended and may be felt, and large-scale parallels may be discerned.

A. *Style from the Viewpoint of Pattern* (*continued*)

5. PROGRESSION IN PATTERN

¶1 Musical motion is given aesthetic reality through progression, as pattern "moves."

¶2 Musical motion is implemented by progression.

¶3 Progression is the manifestation of the primal energy inherent in pattern which imparts to music the quality of advancing motion; SEE TERMS, p. XI.

¶4 Progression is the embodiment of the organic activity implicit in the entire pattern complex.

¶5 Progression is not an abstract attribute of pattern but is dependent on the contribution of the perceiver in thinking and feeling the pattern. [8]

¶6 Progression shows the following aspects:

[5   a. The *field* of progression

¶1 The dimensions of pattern are traversed in the field of progression. [3a]

(1) Motion

(a) Musical motion is distinctive in that nothing moves.

(b) The root and generator of musical motion is pitch motion.

(c) Musical motion comprises pitch change in time, into which is infused qualifying motion of dynamic change.

¶1 Dynamic change inflects the stream of tones in a perspective ranging between dynamic foreground and background. [4b(4a-d)] This changing perspective adds its own dimension of motion and becomes an organic part of the comprehensive motion of pitch-time pattern. [3a]

(d) Pitch, time, and dynamic motion, as aspects of musical motion, enhance one another and form one unique motion.

(e) Musical motion is purely an attribute of pattern in the process of being experienced.

(f) Musical motion is a physical and psychological experience on the part of the perceiver.

(g) The flow of musical motion is reflected in *temporal* and *aesthetic pace*. [5c(7a-b)]

[5a   (2) Time[10]

¶1 Not to be confused with the popular use of "time" to signify "meter."

(a) Musical time is clock time only in the limited sense that music *occurs* in clock time. It is not the mere continuous accretion of pieces of time.

(b) Rather, it is time generated by pattern in motion.

(c) Pattern and the continuum of pitch-time-dynamic motion are one.

(d) The time of pattern is qualitative in nature rather than primarily quantitative. It may therefore properly be called *aesthetic time.*

(e) Clock time is measured by the mechanical process of counting. No objective counting process is involved in measuring aesthetic time. Any physiological or psychological time-measuring process is submerged, in the measuring of time, by the behavior of pattern.

(f) Aesthetic time is measured by the structurally significant moves made as the units of pattern succeed one another. Counting of these moves will gain value only as an aspect of the behavior of pattern, not particularly because of their number, or total, or the apparent exactitude of the count. Time measurement by the behavior of the units of pattern facili-

[10] See Joan Stambaugh, "Music as a Temporal Form," in *The Journal of Philosophy*, Lancaster, Pa., vol. 61, no. 9, Apr. 23, 1964, pp. 265-280.

tates comparisons, as the mechanical measurement of clock time does not.

(g) The time of pattern is manifested tangibly as *structural time*.

(h) For the role of rhythm, a phenomenon of time and pattern, see [3b(2d); 4¶¶2-3]

[5a   (3) Space

¶1 Musical space is the field in which the complex of musical motion manifests itself.

(a) Pitch motion executes pattern as "up-down" motion in an acoustical-psychological *field of pitch change* in the perceiver's imagination.

(b) Pitch motion, however, is at the same time "forward" motion in a *field of time* generated by the pitch motion itself.

(c) The patterned pitch changes, projected into the field of time, are executed coördinately with patterned rhythmic moves in the field of time.

(d) At the same time, pitch-time motion is usually qualified by a concurrent, accessory "foreground-background" motion in a *field of dynamic change*.

(e) The fusion of pitch motion in the field of pitch change with rhythmic motion in the field of time, forms an extended "forward" motion in a *field of linear space*.

(f) These four fields of motion are actually aspects of a single comprehensive field—the *field of musical space*.

¶1 In reference to (a), (b), (d), and (e) above, see [3a]

(g) But, in the generative motion of pitch change, time and linear space become one. [5a(4)]

(h) Musical space unrolls in the imagination of the perceiver through the progression of pattern.

[5a   (4) Extent [5c(9)]

(a) The total aesthetic time generated by pattern is thus a span of imaginative thought.

57

(b) A musical work may therefore be compacted in the imagination into an integrated conception—free from clock time—which facilitates its contemplation as a single aesthetic entity.

(c) The expanse of extent resulting from the elapse of aesthetic time is *aesthetic length*. [5c(9)¶1]

(5) Pace

¶1 Pace is rate of motion.

¶2 For full treatment see [5c(7)]

(a) Temporal pace is the rate of beat motion. [3b (2a)*4, 9*]

(b) Aesthetic pace is the varying rate of progression generated by the qualitative interplay of intensity and detensity in the pattern. [5c(7)¶1]

[5 b. *Engagement of the perceiver* in progression

¶1 For the full experience of the perceiver, see [8-9]

¶2 Participation in progression involves:

(1) Comparison on the part of the perceiver

(a) Comparison is an *activity* of the perceiver in the apperception of pattern.

(b) It is a technique of the mind for fixing and organically associating the elements of pattern.

(c) It is a function of the faculty of relating.

(d) The act of comparison contributes to the energizing of progression in pattern.

1. The progression of pattern advances on a stream of comparisons.

2. Comparison actively reconstructs the relations inherent in pattern.

(e) Comparison is an impulse in all of the processes of progression. [5c]

[5b (2) Expectation on the part of the perceiver

(a) Expectation is an *attitude* of the perceiver in the apperception of pattern.

(b) Stimuli to expectation are inherent in all of the processes of pattern.

(c) Each point of incompletion in the pattern further tends to stimulate expectation.

(e) Each unit of pattern is charged with a quality of impending action which stimulates the advancing motion of progression.

(f) Momentary relaxations of the stimuli to expectation enhance its resumption.

(g) Expectation is an impulse in all of the processes of progression. [5c]

[5b   (3) The contribution of comparison and expectation

(a) The activity of comparison and the attitude of expectation are vehicles indispensable to the perceiver in participating in the processes of progression.

(b) The participation of the perceiver through comparison and expectation is rewarded in the satisfaction achieved in the denouements of progression.

[5c c. The *processes* of progression

¶1 The composer's concept of pattern and expressive effect underlies the formulation of progression.

¶2 The processes of progression are closely interassociated and overlap in their application. They may be grouped as follows:

A. The organic processes of progression

1. Orientation

2. Thematic function (structural)

3. Analogy

4. Proportion

5. Contrast ⎫

6. Integration ⎬ cf. "variety in unity"

B. Processes conditioning the course of progression

7. Aesthetic pace

8. Equilibrium

c. Processes consummating the course of progression

9. Formulation of extent

10. Mood distribution

11. Style distribution

¶3 In later applications of the processes of progression, the above identifying numbering will be maintained.

¶4 The processes of progression are considered in full as follows:

[5c **(1)** *Orientation*

¶1 The value of the term ''orientation'' lies in its comprehension of all types of organization through a basis of reference, whether tonal, modal, or amodal (atonal).

¶2 Some form of referential organization is essential in all styles, even though not focussed on a specific tone of reference.

(a) Tonal and modal orientation

¶1 Orientation in this context is an anticipatory, directional quality in progression, resulting from greater or lesser deference to points of reference in the pattern, inherent or imposed.

¶2 The process of orientation sets up objectives for progression, endowing such points of reference with a quality of attraction (e.g., the tonic, cadential accent)

¶3 Orientation is a fluctuating compensation between centrifugal and centripetal activity, in the ultimate favor of the latter.

1. Points of reference (thrown into relief primarliy by the behavior of the pattern)

a. A tone of reference

b. Moments of reference (rhythmically marked)

c. Mutually supporting correlation of tones and moments of reference.

2. The psychological need of points of reference

a. Based on the principle of economy of perception

b. A tone of reference supplies a focus to the tone pattern.

c. Tones of reference support comparison and expectation and stimulate the sense of progression in the pattern.

d. Accented moments of reference mark the rhythmic features of the pattern and support their correlation.

[5c(1a)   *2e.* The demonstrated point of reference is retained in the perceiver's imagination (unless supplanted by the demonstration of another).

[5c(1d)   *3.* Tendencies toward points of reference

       a. Acoustical tendency

          (1) Subordination to the fundamental by tones in the pattern corresponding to overtones

          (2) Tendency of tones corresponding to overtones to merge with the fundamental by moving to it

          (3) A theory of tendency:[11] of two tones, whose relation is expressed by a ratio from the series of harmonic partials, the one represented by an *even* number is the tone toward which the other tends; e.g.,

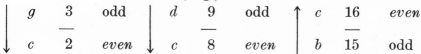

	g	3	odd		d	9	odd		c	16	*even*
	c	2	*even*		c	8	*even*		b	15	odd

¶1 Note that the tendency between the tones of one pitch-class and those of another is accepted by the ear as the same for any tones of the class. Thus the tendency between the tones of a tempered (or other closely approximate interval) is accepted as the same as that between the tones of the corresponding untempered interval, even though the ratio is not exactly the simple ratio of the latter; e.g., in *c-g*, a tempered *g* tends toward *c* as explicitly as an untempered *g*.

          (4) Dominant-like quality of the first overtone

          (5) Dominant-like quality of the overtone series as a whole

[11] Max Friedrich Meyer, ''Contribution to a Psychological Theory of Music,'' in *University of Missouri Studies*, vol. 1, no. 1, Columbia, Mo., 1901.

(6) Chordal skeletons in the overtone series subject to tendency

    (a) Consonant

    (b) Dissonant (including the Skriabin chord in equal temperament)

(7) Acoustical tendency of dissonant combinations to proceed to consonant combinations (resolution)

[5c(1a)*3*   *b.* Rhythmic tendency

    (1) Preëminence of accented beats as orientative points

    (2) Impulse of rising accentuation [4a(2b)*1*]

    (3) Metrical drive

    (4) The impulse of structural rhythm [4c(1d)]

    (5) Completion of the rhythmic motion simultaneously with the arrival of a tone of reference strengthens the orientation.

c. Tendency of nearness

    (1) Half-tone relation

        (a) Tendency of a tone of maximum nearness to merge with a tone of reference by moving to it

        (b) Tendency of a tone dissonant to a tone of reference to resolve to it

    (2) Whole-tone relation

        (a) Tendency of relative nearness

        (b) A strengthened tendency is set up when half- and whole-tone nearnesses combine, in succession or simultaneously.

    (3) 5th relation

        (a) Tendency of the first overtone to move to the fundamental because of its acoustical nearness

[5c(1a)*3*]　　*d.* Tendency of directional motion

　　(1) Tendency to complete the motion in the same direction on approaching a point of reference

　　(2) Tendency to complete scala motion toward a point of reference

　e. Tendency of resolving dissonance
　　(1) Melodic
　　(2) Harmonic
　　(3) Melodic-harmonic
　　(4) Structural [5c(7c)*3e*]

　f. Tendency of expectation

　　(1) In all tendencies the presence of an element of expectation enhances the tendency. [5b(2)]

　g. Multiplied tendency

　　(1) Tendency is increased in proportion to the number and character of associated tendencies.

　　(2) Tendency is especially reinforced by the presence of dissonance and/or rising accentuation.

4. Functioning of the process of orientation

　a. Indication of a point of reference

　　(1) Fixed in the perceiver's imagination by the behavior of the pattern

　　(2) Increased by continued emphasis

　　　(a) Repetitive emphasis
　　　(b) Rhythmic emphasis

　b. Current allusion to a point of reference: Frequent . . . Infrequent

　c. Cumulative directional motion toward it

　d. Anticipation of return to it

　e. Approach to it

　f. Realization of it

63

[5c(1a) *5.* Degree of orientative impulse

    a. Active acoustically and rhythmically (tonality; meter)

    b. Passive acoustically and often rhythmically (modality; measure)

    c. Intermediates

6. The hierarchical character of orientation (relation within relation)

    a. Pitch orientation

        (1) Prime tone of reference

            (a) Tonality

            1' Primary materials (directly functional)

            2' Secondary materials (indirectly functional)

            (b) Modality

            1' Modal T or final (mildly functional)

            2' Modal D (functional in cadences)

            3' Other materials (unfunctional, sometimes weakly functional)

        (2) Sub-tones of reference (tones within the tonal or modal jurisdiction of a prime tone of reference, each exercising its own temporary local influence over other tones, according to the same tendencies as those indicated for prime tones of reference) [5c(1a)*3-5*]

[5c(1a)*6a*   *(3)* Compound tones of reference (prime tones of reference, themselves subject to a chief tone of reference, as in *structural modulation*)

            (a) Systems of key relation in modulation

            1' Principles of *tonal* key relation[12]

                a' In general, the degree of relation of any two keys is based on the correlation of the following factors:

[12] For amplification and qualification of these principles, see Lucille Ravven, *A Study of 18th and 19th Century Tonality,* thesis for the A.M. degree, Vassar College, 1951, pp. 61-74.

64

1' The interval relation of the tonic tones, in the following order of diminishing nearness:

¶1 Cf. [4b(7b)*1a(2c)*]

a' Perfect 5th and 4th
b' Major and minor 3rds
c' Major 2nd
d' Minor 2nd
e' Tritone

2' The quantity of common diatonic material, especially chordal, in the following order of diminishing nearness:

a' Primary chords in common
b' Primary and secondary chords in common
c' Secondary chords in common
d' Gross quantity of chords in common

3' The quantity of non-diatonic material, in the following order of diminishing nearness:

a' Primary chords in conflict
b' Primary and secondary chords in conflict
c' Secondary chords in conflict
d' Gross quantity of chords in conflict

4' Mode homogeneity signifies greater nearness in case other criteria are equivalent.

b' To a large extent, though not with complete consistency in different historical situations, composers' practices support the above theoretical system.

2' Principles of *modal* "key" relation

    a' In general, the degree of relation of any two modal "keys" is indeterminate, except that the historical trend is toward the practice of tonal relations.

        1' The interval relation of the tones of reference of any two modal "keys" is in the following order of increasing nearness:

¶1 Cf. [4b(7b)*1b(2c)*]

            a' Major and (sometimes) minor 2nds

            b' Minor and major 3rds

            c' Perfect 4ths and 5ths

    b' Resources of modal modulation

        1' Modulation from one mode to a different mode in the same diatonic gamut (e.g., from D Dorian to E Phrygian)

        2' Modulation from one mode to the same mode in a different diatonic gamut (e.g., from D Dorian to A Dorian)

        3' Modulation from one mode to a different mode in a different diatonic gamut (e.g., C Ionian to F Ionian)

[5c(1a)*6a(3)*   *(b)* Modulatory function

      1' Structural modulation

      2' Color modulation

      3' Combination

    (c) Modulatory pace

      1' Intense

        a' Relatively frequent modulation

        b' Relatively many keys: Rapidly reached . . . Slowly reached

        c' Relatively distant keys: Rapidly
        reached (cf. e.g., the side-slip) . . .
        Slowly reached
        d' Mixtures

[5c(1a)*6a(3c)*]   2' Detense
        a' Relatively infrequent modulation
        b' Relatively few keys
        c' Relatively near keys: Rapidly
        reached . . . Slowly reached
        d' Mixtures

    b. Rhythmic orientation

1. Compound points of reference in structural rhythm [4c(1d)*3*]

2. Attraction of the rhythmically emphasized objective in structural rhythm

3. Graduated analogical relations of hierarchal rhythmic factors [5c(3b)*2*; 5c(3d)*1*]

7. The scope of orientation
    a. Local melodic/rhythmic/harmonic orientation
    b. Local structural/rhythmic orientation
    c. Extensive structural orientation
    d. Orientation in the cycle

8. The comprehensive pattern of orientation is an intrinsic part of the larger organic structure.

[5c(1)   (b) Amodal (atonal) orientation

¶1 Amodal styles reveal specialized forms of referential organization, which provide their own quality of orientation.

    1. Bases of reference
        a. The pattern unit as a basis of reference (a motive, phrase, or *ostinato* detail, in noticeable relief, later touched upon or returned to, sometimes at the same pitch)
        b. Local bases of reference (tones or pattern units established, and referred to momentarily, in support of local, temporary orientation)

67

c. The tonerow as a substratum of reference (the submerged but pervasive *ostinato* quality of the tonerow as an orientative force in extensive passages or entire structures)

d. Rhythmic pattern of a serial rhythm as a point of reference

e. Rhythmically marked points of reference

2. The psychological need of bases of reference; cf. [5c(1a)*2*]

3. Rhythmic tendency toward points of reference; cf. [5c(1a)*3b*]

4. Degree of orientative impulse

a. Neutral acoustically; often active rhythmically (amodality; meter, mixed meter, irregular meter, polymeter)

5. Transposition of the tonerow [4c(2h)*3*] is analogous to modulation; cf [5c(1a)*6a(3)*]

6. The scope of orientation; cf. [5c(1a)*7*]

7. The comprehensive pattern of orientation is an intrinsic part of the larger organic structure; cf. [5c(1a)*8*]

[5c(1)   (c) Intermediate or mixed orientation

¶1 Devices of tonal and amodal orientation may be associated in mutual support.

[5c   (2) *Thematic function*

¶1 Thematic function is the characteristic behavior of thematic ideas or areas, in shaping and individualizing the structure.

¶2 Thematic functions are interdependent and in part owe their identity to context.

[5c(2)   (a) The thematic functions

1. Pre-exposition (the tentative foreshadowing of a thematic idea before its definitive exposition; cf. *10.* Introduction below and note the difference)

2. Exposition (the first definitive presentation of a thematic idea)

3. Counter-exposition (the exposition of a thematic idea or area introduced as suitable contrast to a particular previous exposition)

¶1 Counter-exposition is usually reinforced by change in tonal or other orientation.

4. Exposition restated (the more or less exact reprise of a thematic idea or area after contrast)

¶1 Reprise is usually reinforced by the return, at the same time, of the main point of orientation.

5. Exposition reformulated (the reconsideration in reprise of an earlier exposition, usually developmental and often involving a resultant asymmetry in the larger structure)

[5c(2a)] *6.* The variant (the re-presentation of a thematic idea, or part of an idea, with modifications, which nevertheless leave the source recognizably intact; related in invention to development, though relatively static in itself)

7. Transformation (change in the character and expressive effect of a thematic idea, while retaining enough of the original idea for reminder)

8. Relevant continuation (the local expansion of a thematic idea short of the higher evolving progression of development)

9. Development (the organic evolution and exploitation of a thematic idea)

¶1 Development is reinforced by progressing changes in tonal or other orientation.

[5c(2a)] *10.* Introduction (a prefatory thematic idea or passage, leading with anticipation to a definitive thematic exposition)

11. Approach (structural rising inflection [4c(1d) 1c], building up to and projected into a point of structural weight, e.g., a reprise; cf. *1.* Preexposition above)

69

12. Extension (structural falling inflection [4c(1d) *1c*] ; an appended after-idea, continuing its predecessor toward completion)

13. Conclusion (a passage or area reinforcing and bringing to a positive close its predecessor or predecessors)

14. Transition (a passage of specifically connective, dependent character, leading from one relatively more important passage to another)

15. Interpolation (an episodical passage or area introduced as relief between two more basic passages or areas)

[5c(2)   (b) Functional attributes of thematic ideas

     1. Predictive (stimulating expectation)
       a. Pre-exposition
       b. Introduction
       c. Approach
       d. Transition

     2. Assertive (the basis of comparison)
       a. Exposition
       b. Counter-exposition

     3. Exploitive (stimulating comparison and expectation)
       a. Variant
       b. Transformation
       c. Relevant continuation
       d. Development

     4. Confirmative (stimulating comparison)
       a. Exposition restated
       b. Exposition reformulated
       c. Extension
       d. Conclusion

     5. Digressive
       a. Transition
       b. Interpolation

70

[5c(2)] (c) Each thematic function involves a special and idiosyncratic formulation of pattern and logic, and a specialized manipulation of tensity.

(d) Degree of tensity of the functional qualities and of their interaction in application: Intense . . . Detense

(e) Hierarchal relations among themes in shaping the structure (based on the manipulation of themes in a scale of relative thematic values) [4a(4d)]

   1. Primary
      a. Thematic idea
      b. Companion idea
   2. Secondary
      a. Attending idea
      b. Ancillary idea
   3. Tertiary
      a. Subordinate tone-line
      b. Intermittent filler

[5c(2)] (f) The thematic functions interrelate and may somewhat overlap.

(g) One function may be contained within another (e.g., development within exposition).

(h) All thematic functions may be manifested locally (e.g., extension of a division), or extensively (e.g., a final coda to the work as a whole).

(j) Various arrangements and emphases among the functions are influential in the progression of the structure toward its individual shape.

(k) Manipulation of the thematic functions contributes to the process of integration [5c(6)], in association with the course of the aesthetic pace. [5c(7)]

(m) The comprehensive pattern of the thematic functions influences the character and underlies the individuality of the larger structure.

[5c] (3) *Analogy*[13]

[13] See the author's ''Analogical Relations in Musical Pattern,'' in *The Journal of Aesthetics and Art Criticism,* vol. 17, no. 1, September 1958, pp. 77-84; re-

¶1 Analogy is the logical progression from an original unit or process of pattern, to a succeeding unit (or succession of units), or to an enlargement of a process of pattern, through the incorporation of a *significant difference* between analogue and original; cf. [5c(6)]

(a) Relations of the analogue to the original in structure
1. Near-reproduction
2. Confirmation
3. Complementation
4. Antithesis
5. Variant
6. Continuation
7. Completion
8. Reflection
9. Development
10. Overlapping and mingled relations

[5c(3)]   (b) Orders of analogy in structure
1. Simple analogy
   a. Paired relation (periodic; chiefly in linear structure)
   (1) Near reproduction
   (2) Confirmation
   (3) Complementation
   (4) Antithesis
   (5) Variant
   (6) Completion
   (7) Reflection

   b. Chain relation (relevant continuation of the original by several analogues)

   c. Variant relation (addition of a succession of variant analogues)

[5c(3b)]   *d.* The relation of evolving succession (developmental analogues)

printed in *Journal of the American Musicological Society*, vol. 13, 1960, pp. 224-261.

2. Graduated analogy

    a. Compound relation (span within span, the greater containing the lesser)

    b. Successive relation (span following span, the greater following the lesser)

[5c(*3*)]   (c) Applications of analogy in structure

¶1 The applications of analogy are stated below in the order from lesser to greater extent; those of greatest extent are integral forms.

    1. Immediate analogy

       a. Linear application

          (1) Paired relation

            (a) Repeat (weak pair)

            (b) Period

            (c) Double period

            (d) Binary-form

          (2) Chain relation

            (a) Sequence (transposed repeats or near-repeats)

              1' Melodic

              2' Harmonic

              3' Structural (modulatory)

            (b) Cursive succession (relevant continuation)

            (c) Cursive-form

          (3) Variant relation

            (a) Variant phrase analogy (local)

            (b) Variation-form

[5c(3c)*1*]   *b. Polylinear* application

          (1) Thematic exchange (*Stimmtausch;* rondellus-form) [4c(2d)*1*]

          (2) Isorhythmic structure [4c(2h)*5*]

          (3) Successive imitation

            (a) Fugal exposition (fugue-form)

            (b) Approximate imitation

(4) Overlapping imitation (canon)
   (a) Canonic exposition (fuga-form, as in the canzona ricercar)
   (b) Canon-form

(5) Analogy by thematic mutation
   (a) Augmentation
   (b) Diminution
   (c) Inversion
   (d) Retrograde

(6) Ostinato (against changing context)

(7) Analogy by imitation and overlap of the original and analogue: stretto (may combine with analogy by thematic mutation)

2. Deferred analogy: *linear* application (analogical comparison resuming after digression or contrast)
   a. Binary-form (with terminal reversion)
   b. Cursive-form (with terminal reversion)
   c. Ternary-form
[5c(3c)*2*   *d.* Rondo-form
   e. Bowed rondo-form
   f. Sonata-form
   g. Bowed sonata-form

[5c(3)   (d) Non-structural analogy (compound), in—

   1. Rhythm
     a. Rising accentuation, e.g.,

Weaker beat	: Stronger beat
:: Weaker accent-group	: Stronger accent-group
Weaker phrase-accent	: Stronger phrase-accent
:: Weaker period	: Stronger period
Lesser cadence	: Greater cadence
:: Greater cadence	: Still greater cadence
Lesser climax	: Greater climax
:: Greater climax	: Still greater climax

b. Falling accentuation, e.g.,

Suspension or
  retardation   : Resolution
:: Accented part of   : Unaccented part of
  feminine ending   feminine ending

Cadential expansion : Local extension
:: Penultimate close   : Coda

[5c(3d)]   *2.* Tonal orientation

a. Tonal cadence relations, e.g.,
V   : I
:: Dom. key modulation : Ton. return
:: Dom. structural   :Ton. structural
  division   division

b. Tonal harmonic functions, e.g.,
II   :   V
V   :   I

c. Tonal key functions, e.g.,
Dom. key   : Ton. key
:: Dom. group   : Ton. group

Sub-dom. key   : Ton. key
:: Sub-dom. coda   : Final ton. conclusion

[5c(3d)]   *3.* Tensity, e.g.,
Dissonance   : Consonance
:: Climax preparation : Climax resolution and
  and denouement   denouement
:: Larger structural   : Larger structural
  dissonance   resolution [5c(7c)*3e*]

[5c(3d)]   *4.* Nuance, e.g.,
Crescendo   : Decrescendo
:: Climax approach   : Climax resolution

Local ritardando   : Terminal allargando
:: Locally inflective   : Structural rubato
  rubato

[15d(2c)]

75

5. Thematic functions, e.g.,

    a. Lesser exposition within greater exposition

    b. Lesser development within greater exposition or development

    c. Lesser conclusion within greater exposition or conclusion
    etc.

[5c(3)] (e) The comprehensive pattern of analogy emerges from the cumulative relations of the individual analogies in formulation of the larger pattern.

[5c] (4) *Proportion*

¶1 Proportion is the relation of lengths of structural span, temporal and aesthetic, in balance and imbalance in progression. [5c(9)¶1; 5c(9a)]

¶2 Balance may be secured by equivalent aesthetic length as well as by equal temporal length. [5c(9a)]

¶3 As used here in connection with proportion, "regular" implies "symmetrical" and "irregular" "asymmetrical."

  (a) Comparison of span lengths

    1. Temporal length

    2. Aesthetic length (temporal length qualified by tensity)

  (b) Symmetry (balance of spans)

    1. Balance in temporal length

    2. Balance in aesthetic length

  (c) Asymmetry (contrived balance or controlled imbalance of spans, —referable to the perceiver's image of symmetry as a basis of comparison)

[5c(4)] (d) Distribution of spans

    1. Adjacent spans

      a. Symmetry (e.g., binary-form)

      b. Asymmetry (e.g., expanded binary-form)

    2. Spans separated by intervening divisions of structure

      a. Symmetry (e.g., ternary-form, basic sonata-form)

76

b. Bowed symmetry (e.g., bowed sonata-form)

c. Asymmetry (e.g., expanded ternary-form, expanded sonata-form)

(e) Tensity in span relation, resulting from—

1. Pulse against counterpulse between spans in regular proportion (structural rising or falling accentuation)

2. Asymmetry against symmetry between spans in irregular proportion

[5c(4)   (f) The comprehensive pattern of proportions is influential in determining the balance of tensities and shape of the larger structure.

[5c   (5) *Contrast*

¶1 Contrast is the interplay of similarity and dissimilarity among the properties and activities of pattern in progression.
¶2 Diversity is contingent on a prevailing homogeneity into which to introduce the diversity. Such relative homogeneity is a requisite to aesthetic value. [5c(11g)]
¶3 The pattern of contrast governs the variety in "Variety in unity."

(a) The quality of contrast is dependent on the range and rate of change.

1. Range of change: Wide . . . Narrow

2. Rate of change: Immediate (rhetorical or dramatic) . . . Gradual (evolving)

3. Combinations

¶1 Innumerable combinations of range and rate give contrast great versatility.

4. The manipulation of the range and rate of change implements aesthetic pace, in which the quality of contrast is reflected. [5c(7)]

[5c(5)   (b) The province of contrast

¶1 The factors implementing contrast may operate locally or extensively.

1. Contrast in idiom

   a. Local and temporary inflections of the idiom itself

   b. Basic contrast of idiom as a part of the comprehensive structural and stylistic pattern

2. Contrast in the elements of pattern

   a. Melody/rhythm

      (1) Contrast inherent in the tensities of melodic progression

      (2) Contrast induced among successive or simultaneous melodic ideas

   b. Texture (including harmony)/rhythm

      (1) Contrast inherent in the tensities of textural progression

      (2) Contrast introduced in the course of the changing textural pattern

   c. Structure/rhythm

      (1) Contrast inherent in the diversification of points of reference

      (2) Contrast inherent in the diversification of thematic ideas

      (3) Contrast inherent in the diversification of the relations of analogues to originals

      (4) Contrast in the manipulation of symmetry and asymmetry

      (5) Contrast inherent in the manipulation of the process of logical expansion

      (6) Contrast in the diversification of tensities

      (7) Contrast in the manipulation of imbalances and compensations

[5c(5b)   *3.* Dynamic contrast

   a. Local contrast

      (1) Immediate

        (a) Accent

        (b) Rhetorical emphasis

78

        (2) Gradual (nuance)

    b. Extensive contrast (involving structure and style)

        (1) Structural rhetorical emphasis

        (2) Dramatic emphasis

        (3) Climax preparation and resolution

        (4) The larger dynamic pattern

  4. Timbre contrast

    a. Within one medium

    b. Among media (orchestration)

[5c(5) (c) Contrast in the functioning of the processes of progression

¶1 The processes of progression most involved are:

1. Orientation [5c(1)]: contrast through the diversification of points of reference

2. Thematic function [5c(2)]: contrast through the diversification of thematic ideas

3. Analogy [5c(3)]: contrast through the diversification of the relations of analogues to originals

4. Proportion [5c(4)]: contrast through the manipulation of symmetry and asymmetry

7. Aesthetic pace [5c(7)]: contrast through the diversification of tensities

8. Equilibrium [5c(8)]: contrast through the manipulation of imbalances and compensations

10. Mood distribution [5c(10)]: contrast through the diversification of moods

11. Style distribution [5c(11)]: contrast through the diversification of styles

(d) The comprehensive pattern of contrast, based on the range and rate of change, inflects every aspect of the complex of pattern, expressive effect, and style.

[5c (6) *Integration*

¶1 Integration is the progression of pattern to form an

79

organic whole, by means of the processes of the specialized logic of music.[14]

¶2 Integration is the agency of unity in "variety in unity."

(a) Integration involves an association of deductive and inductive musical logic.

1. Deduction in progressing pattern is the musically reasoned process of inferring succeeding steps in the pattern from an original assertion and from one another; cf. [5c(3)]

2. Induction in progressing pattern is the musically reasoned process of pre-projecting the extensive pattern from the emerging constituent parts; cf. [5c(9)]

(b) The deductive process proceeds through—

1. The cumulative stages of analogical comparison [5c(3)]

2. The inherently expansive process of development involving—

a. Selection of thematic ingredients for treatment

b. Formulation of expanding successions of relatively unstable consequents extracted from the thematic ingredients

c. Formulation of substantially new consequents, nevertheless showing relation to the original thematic ingredients

[5c(6)] (c) The inductive process proceeds through—

1. The projection of the comprehensive pattern of aesthetic pace from the local fluctuations of tensity [5c(7)]

2. The projection of the comprehensive equilibrium from the imbalances of the parts [5c(8)]

3. The projection of the shape of the comprehensive

[14] For a treatment of the detail of musical logic, see Charles Seeger, ''On the Moods of a Music Logic,'' in *Journal of the American Musicological Society:* A Musicological Offering to Otto Kinkeldey, vol. 13, 1960, pp. 224-261.

extent from the interplay of local quantitative and qualitative lengths [5c(9)]

4. The projection of the complex of the whole from the inherently simpler parts

5. The projection of completion from the incompletion of the parts [5c(6d)]

[5c(6)]   (d) Integration through the progression of relative incompletion toward completion

¶1 The processes of progression most involved are:

1. Orientation [5c(1)]: completion (modal, tonal, or other) through the cumulative succession of points of reference

2. Thematic function [5c(2)]: Completion through the course pursued by the thematic functions

a. Exposition: tentative or local completion

b. Exposition restated (reprise): confirmed completion

c. Conclusion: confirmed completion

d. Development: active incompletion

e. Approach, pre-exposition, introduction, transition: tentative incompletion

3. Analogy [5c(3)]: completion through the analogical multiplication of units

7. Aesthetic pace [5c(7)]: completion through the comprehensive resolution of tensities

a. Structural tensity and resolution
b. Climax tensity and resolution
c. Mood tensity and resolution

8. Equilibrium [5c(8)]: completion through the compensation of imbalances

[5c(6)]   (e) Momentum in integration

¶1 Momentum is the tendency of progression to continue to advance, arising both from the processes introduced in the pattern which imply or demand completion, and from the expectation induced by the initiation of such processes (e.g.,

81

sequence, orientative organization, climax preparation and resolution, etc.).

¶2 Momentum is a corollary of integration.

    1. The sources of momentum
        a. The insistent nature of pattern in motion
        b. The compelling logic of integration
        c. Temporal pace
        d. Aesthetic pace [5c(7)]

[5c(6e)]   *2.* The elements of pattern conveying momentum

    a. Melody/rhythm: the pursuit of the convolutions of the melodic contour, supported by the propulsion of its rhythm and tensities, and by the impulses of orientation, conveys momentum.

    b. Texture/rhythm: the functional harmonic progressions, supported by the propulsion of their rhythm and tensities, and by the impulses of orientation, convey momentum.

    c. Structure/rhythm: all of the comparative processes of structural progression, the pulse and counter-pulse of structural rhythm, and the impulses of orientation, convey momentum.

[5c(6)]   (f) Cumulation in integration

¶1 Cumulation is the quality of increasing conviction in the logical relations of the parts and elements of pattern, in their progression toward and denouement in the comprehensive pattern of extent. [5c(9)]

¶2 Cumulation is a corollary of integration.

    (g) Inertia in integration

¶1 Inertia is marked by lack of an appreciable sense of advance, as seen in—

    1. Static passages (cf. the inertness of some manifestations of modality)

    2. Local passages of intentional contra-integration [5c(6j)]

    3. Extensive passages of inadvertent contra-integration, involving impairment of the logic of integration [5c(6j)]

(h) The comprehensive pattern of integration forms the core of the larger structure.

[5c(6)]   (j) Contra-integration

¶1 Cf. [5c(6g)]

¶2 Contra-integration (except in logically inept music) is a calculated temporary deviation from the logically expected continuity of progression.

¶3 Deviations create expectation to be satisfied by their consequent justification.

¶4 Deviations may be the consequence of and justified by delineative or descriptive intention. [6b(1)]

¶5 Aesthetically convincing deviations are assimilated and contribute a measure of stimulation and individuality to the pattern.

¶6 The deviations of contra-integration are as follows:

[5c(6j)]   *1.* Suspense of the integrative logic

    a. Rhetorical interruption

    b. Ellipsis, hiatus

    2. Deflection of the logic

    a. Discontinuity

    b. Exclamatory rhetoric

    c. Fragmentation

    3. Lapse of the logic

    a. Hesitation

    b. Dissolution of the pattern

    4. Resumption of the logic

[5c]   (7) *Aesthetic pace*[16]

¶1 Aesthetic pace is the varying rate of progression generated by the qualitative interplay of intensity and detensity in the pattern.

(a) The field of aesthetic pace

    1. Temporal pace, and its collateral, temporal

[15] See the author's ''Aesthetic Pace in Music,'' in *The Journal of Aesthetics and Art Criticism*, vol. 15, no. 3, March 1957, pp. 311-321.

length, are quantitative prefigurations of *aesthetic pace* and *aesthetic length.*

2. Aesthetic pace and aesthetic length are qualitative aspects of pattern.

3. Aesthetic pace and aesthetic length underlie the qualitative phenomenon of extent. [5c(9)]

(b) The qualitative character of aesthetic pace

1. Product of the manipulation of the tensities of pattern

2. Product of the manipulation of the range and rate of contrast in numerous combinations

[5c(7)] (c) Changes of tensity, implementing aesthetic pace, take place in—

1. Melody/rhythm

a. Tensity pattern of the pitch contour: Conjunction . . . Angularity, Consonance . . . Dissonance

b. Relation of the rhythmic pattern to the beatgroup: Agreement . . . Disagreement

c. Tensity pattern in the proportion of tones outside the mode to those within the mode: Diatonic . . . Chromatic

d. Tensity pattern in the pitch and rhythmic configuration: Essential tone-line . . . Decorated tone-line

2. Texture/rhythm (including harmony)

a. Linear aspect of texture

(1) Harmonic/rhythmic progression

(a) Tensity pattern of consonance-dissonance: Consonance . . . Dissonance

(b) Tensity pattern in the proportion of tones outside the mode to those within the mode: Diatonic . . . Chromatic

[5c(7c)2] *(c)* Tensity pattern of harmonic progression: Active progression . . . Passive pro-

84

gression, Frequent progression . . . Infrequent progression

(d) Tensity pattern of harmonic rhythm: Active . . . Passive

[5c(7c)*2a*   *(2)* Textural/rhythmic activity

(a) Tensity of the textural mass (increase or decrease in the number of simultaneous tones): Thickening . . . Thinning

(b) Tensity in the spread of the tone lines: Opening . . . Closing

(c) Tensity in the cross-activity among lines: Marked . . . Limited

(d) Tensity pattern of melodic-harmonic consonance-dissonance: Non-chord tones few (especially accented tones) . . . Non-chord tones many (especially accented tones)

(e) Tensity based on the introduction of polyphonic activity: Marked . . . Limited

b. Polylinear aspect of texture

(1) Tensities of the individual lines

(2) Tensities among the interacting lines

(c) Tensity of rhythmic counteractivity

(d) Tensity pattern of consonance-dissonance

(5) Tensity in the opening and closing of texture

(6) Tensity pattern of melodic-harmonic consonance-dissonance (within the harmonic frame of polyphony)

[5c(7c)   *3.* Structure/rhythm

a. Degrees of structural tensity in the idiom

(1) Linear structure tends to be relatively less intense than polylinear (but cf. incorporated tensity). [5c(9h)*2-3*]

¶1 The presence of tensity in linear structure may come also from various tensities other than structural.

(2) Polylinear structure tends to be relatively more intense than linear structure.

b. Degrees of structural tensity in the form-type
   (1) Intrinsic [5c(9h)*1*]
   (2) Incorporated [5c(9h)*2-3*]

c. Structural tensity through the suspense contributed by climax[16]
   (1) The course of climax
      (a) Preparation: Long . . . Short
      (b) Approach: Long . . . Short
      (c) Culmination: Long . . . Short
      (d) Postponement
      (e) Interruption
      (f) Resolution: Immediate . . . Gradual
      (g) Anti-climax (arrested climax)

   (2) Degrees of tensity of climax: Intensity . . . Detensity

[5c(7c)*3c*]   *(3)* Levels of climax
      (a) Simple
      (b) Compound
         1' Lesser climax within greater climax
         2' Lesser climax leading to greater climax

   (4) Influence of the placement of climax on the form-type

¶1 The character of a given form-type may be modified by different placements of climax.

      (a) Typical placements
         1' Tapering treatment of the form-type: placement of the main climax, marking the high point of intensity, somewhat after the mid-point of the form

         2' Cumulative treatment of the form-type: placement of the main climax, mark-

[16] Cf. William S. Newman, ''The Climax of Music,'' in *Extension Bulletin*, University of North Carolina, vol. 31, no. 3, January 1952.

ing the high point of intensity, at the end of the form

(b) The placement of climax collaborates with other factors of tensity in the pattern.

(c) The main climax is the tensity crisis of the form.

[5c(7c)*3*   *d.* Tensity of structural progression toward increased complexity

(1) This is an organic form of tensity.

(2) A point of complexity may constitute an intense organic pattern climax with or without parallel support from other tensities (e.g., increase in dynamics or pace).

e. Interplay of structural tensities

¶1 The interplay of various structural tensities between intensity and detensity may be considered as—

(1) Structural dissonance
(2) Structural resolution

4. Dynamics and timbre

a. Changes in the tensity of pattern are enhanced by supporting changes in the tensity of dynamics and timbre.

b. Changes in the tensities of dynamics and timbre may occur separately or in collaboration.

c. Changes in the tensities of dynamics and timbre become an intrinsic part of the pattern.

[5c(7)   (d) Tensive effect of the processes of progression on aesthetic pace

¶1 The processes of progression most involved are:

1. Orientation [5c(1)]

a. Degrees of tensity inherent in the tone system

(1) Tonality is relatively intense
(2) Modality is relatively detense
(3) Amodality is maximally intense

b. Manipulation of the degrees of orientative tensity: Active . . . Passive

87

[5c(7d)] *2.* Thematic function [5c(2)]

¶1 Several of the thematic functions contribute to the quality of tensity, some of them through their sense of incompletion. Those most assertive are:

a. Variant
b. Development
c. Introduction
d. Approach
e. Transition

4. Proportion [5c(4)]

a. Prevailingly regular proportion is relatively detense.

b. Prevailingly irregular proportion is relatively intense.

5. Contrast [5c(5)]

a. The increase and decrease of contrast make for changing degrees of tensity.

6. Integration [5c(6)]

a. The quality of momentum in integration makes for intensity.

b. The quality of cumulation makes for intensity.

10. Mood distribution [5c(10)]

a. Changes in pattern stimulating different moods make for changing degrees of tensity.

11. Style distribution

a. Changes in pattern stimulating differences in style make for changing degrees of tensity. [5c(11)]

[5c(7)] (e) Tensity in aesthetic pace occasioned by suspense, through—

1. Integrative drive

2. Manipulation of the function of development

3. Manipulation of the function of approach (e.g., to a reprise)

4. Manipulation of modulation

88

5. Preparation and approach to the culmination of climax

6. Quality of incompletion [5c(6d)]

7. Rhetorical interruption

8. Insistent continuity (particularly when associated with several of the above forms of suspense)

(f) Interplay of tensities in aesthetic pace

1. The particular association of different kinds of tensity at a given point determines—

    a. The degree of emphasis on tensity

    b. The rate of the aesthetic pace at that point

2. The various kinds of tensity may be associated in—

    a. Many different combinations

    b. Many relative emphases

3. The larger pattern of tensities correlates with aesthetic pace itself.

(g) Consequence of aesthetic pace to expressive effect

1. The pattern of aesthetic pace is collateral with mood distribution.

2. Differentiation of expressive effect through aesthetic pace

    a. Detense aesthetic pace: *lyric* effect, characterized by—

        (1) Homogeneity of the processes of pattern

        (2) Relatively restricted contrast

[5c(7g)*2a*]   *(3)* Relatively restricted rhetorical effects

        (4) Homogeneity of style

        (5) Homogeneity of mood

    b. Intense aesthetic pace: *dramatic* effect, characterized by—

        (1) Diversified processes of pattern

        (2) Relative emphasis on contrast

        (3) Marked use of rhetorical effects

(4) Diversity of mood

(5) Diversity of style

c. Variable aesthetic pace: *lyrico-dramatic* effect, characterized by a pattern mingling the qualities of the lyric and the dramatic

[5c(7)   (h) The attributes of aesthetic pace

1. Aesthetic pace is a reflection of the changing tensities of musical motion.

2. Aesthetic pace is a reflection of the changing impulses of progression.

3. Aesthetic pace is a reflection of the individuality of pattern and expressive effect.

4. Aesthetic pace furnishes the distinctions between the lyric and the dramatic.

5. Aesthetic pace is the index of the changing current of expressive effect.

6. Aesthetic pace operates in the province of extent. [5c(9)]

(j) The comprehensive pattern of aesthetic pace influences the shaping of the pattern and expressive effect of the whole work.

[5c   (8) *Equilibrium*

¶1 Equilibrium is the result of the compensation of imbalances among the properties and activities of pattern in progression.

(a) Compensations in the course of the pattern resolve the imbalances inherent in the processes of progression; all of the processes are involved:

1. Orientation [5c(1)]: the anticipatory and integrative tendencies of orientation are resolved in the succession of arrivals at the proposed pitch, time, and structural points of reference.

2. Thematic function [5c(2)]: the characteristic tendencies of the thematic functions are resolved in the responding shape and individualization of the structure.

3. Analogy [5c(3)]: the interplay of originals and analogues is resolved in the completion of the cumulative analogical pattern.

4. Proportion [5c(4)]: the interplay of symmetry and asymmetry is resolved in the nominal assimilation of asymmetry within a comprehensive symmetry.

5. Contrast [5c(5)]: the interplay of similarity and diversity is resolved in the unifying force of integration and in the patterned changes of aesthetic pace.

6. Integration [5c(6)]: the insistence of integration to fulfill its logical course is resolved in the conviction of the resultant pattern.

[5c(8a)] *7.* Aesthetic pace [5c(7)]: the interplay of intensity and detensity is resolved in an ultimate aesthetic repose.[17]

8. Extent [5c(9)]: the interplay of the quantitative and qualitative aspects of extent is resolved in the resultant absorption of the former by the latter.

9. Mood distribution [5c(10)]: the interplay of the lyric and the dramatic is resolved in the comprehensive lyric frame of the work as a whole. [8h(4)]

10. Style distribution [5c(11)]: the interplay of style contrasts is resolved in the comprehensive style homogeneity of the work as a whole. [5c(11g)]

[5c(8)] (b) Equilibrium varies in the degree of its influence.

1. A degree of uncompensated imbalance is inherent in romantic style.

2. A prevailing compensation of imbalance is inherent in classic style.

3. A degree of uncompensated imbalance is inherent in dramatic style.

[17] See Ethel D. Puffer, *The Psychology of Beauty*, Boston & New York, 1905, pp. 77-79.

4. A prevailing compensation of imbalance is inherent in lyric style.

(c) The comprehensive pattern of equilibrium underlies the aesthetic repose of the work as a whole. [5c(8a)7]

[5c (9) *Formulation of extent*

¶1 Extent is the product of progression in aesthetic time [5a(2f)], resulting in aesthetic length [5a(4c)], and in a qualitatively defined attribute—the *extensity* of the work as a whole.

(a) Measurement of extent [5a(2, 4)]

1. Measured elementarily and literally in clock time and characterized by temporal pace and length

2. Measured significantly in structural time and characterized by aesthetic pace and length

a. A qualitative measure based on the tensity pattern of the given extent

b. The tensity pattern is reflected in the aesthetic pace.

(b) The tensive quality of extent

1. The basis of tensity lies in the range and rate of contrast; as in [5c(5c)]

2. Factors affording contrast; as in [5c(5b)]

3. The interplay of intensity and detensity generates the quality of extensity.

(c) Impulses generating extent [5c(1-8, 10-11)]

¶1 All of the processes of progression are involved in generating extent.

(d) The scope of extent

1. Component units of structure: Short span . . . Long span

2. Integral structural extent: Short span . . . Long span

3. Composite structural extent: Short span . . . Long span

[5c(9)   (e) The graduation of extent
   1. Marked contrast (dramatic)
      a. Local rhetorical effect
      b. Extensive evolving contrast
      c. Diversity of mood
      d. Diversity of style

   2. Limited contrast (lyric)
      a. Homogeneity of mood
      b. Concentration of mood
      c. Concentration of style

   3. Mingled degrees of contrast

   4. Wide extent requires marked variety.

   5. Slight extent requires limited variety.

[5c(9)   (f) The indeterminate character of extent
   1. The apparent expanse of extent lies in a balance between its temporal and aesthetic lengths.

   2. The more intense the processes of pattern are, the less expanse the extent seems to cover. [5c(7g) *2b*]

   3. The more detense the processes of pattern are, the greater expanse the extent seems to cover. [5c(7g)*2a*]

   (g) Regulation of extent
   1. Linear structure
      a. Prolongation is precluded when further intensity or detensity would approach the deterioration of the progression.
      b. The introduction of a new division or movement tends to signalize a necessary or desirable limitation of the previous span of extent.

   2. Polylinear structure
   ¶1 The regulation of extent in polylinear structure corresponds to that in linear structure, with the exception given in *a* below:

93

a. The inherent intensity of polylinear structure and its preoccupation with local interlinear processes tend to limit its spans of extent, as compared with those of linear structure.

b. Since the processes of polylinear structure do not fully lend themselves to extensity, as compared with those of linear structure, greater extents can be secured only by the cursive addition of divisions, sometimes at the price of looseness in the larger linear structure.

[5c(9)] (h) Adjustment of extent in the conventional forms [4c(1h)*3e*; 4c(2j)3b]

    1. Extent of normal *intrinsic* tensity

      a. Low-tensity forms

        (1) Homophony

          (a) Period-form

          (b) Stanza-form

          (c) Variation-form

        (2) Polyphony

          (a) *Cantus firmus*-based form

          (b) Canon-form

[5c(9h)*1*] *b.* Middle tensity forms

        (1) Homophony

          (a) Binary-form

          (b) Ternary-form

          (c) Rondo-form

        (2) Polyphony

          (a) Cursive-form

          (b) Fuga-form

      c. High tensity forms

        (1) Homophony

          (a) Sonata-form

          (b) Rondo sonata-form

          (c) Bowed sonata-form

        (2) Polyphony

          (a) Fugue-form, simple

          (b) Fugue-form, multithematic

[5c(9h)] *2.* Extent qualitatively changed by *incorporated* tensity above or below the norm

    a. Intensity produced by *pronounced*—

        (1) Thematic tensity

        (2) Development

        (3) Continuity

        (4) Polyphonic interest

        (5) Asymmetry

        (6) Climax emphasis

        (7) Progression complexity

        (8) Mood contrast

        (9) Style contrast

    b. Detensity produced by *intrusive*—

        (1) Repetition

        (2) Sectionality

        (3) Variety

        (4) Lack of correlation among the thematic ideas

        (5) Rhetorical interruption

        (6) Dramatic contrast

        (7) Mood contrast

        (8) Style contrast

3. Extent qualitatively changed by *changed temporal length* above or below the norm (may enhance or impair)

    a. Temporal length reduced in relation to tensity: super-compact structure

    b. Temporal length increased in relation to tensity: super-spread structure

[5c(9)]   (j) Conformation of extent to different criteria

    1. Adaptation to classic criteria (e.g., the architectonic sonata-form)

    2. Adaptation to romantic criteria (e.g., the lyric sonata-form)

    3. Adaptation to the criteria of program music and music drama (e.g., the dramatic and delineative sonata-form)

[5c(9) (k) The comprehensive pattern of extent is the core of the pattern of the work as a whole.

[5c(10) *Mood distribution*

¶1 Mood distribution concerns the character of, succession of, and emphasis among, the moods evoked by pattern, and is an impulse in the progression of aesthetic pace.

(a) The character of mood is in part preconceived by the composer, in part shaped concurrently with his evolution of the pattern.

(b) Mood is the consequence, in the perceiver's experience, of his sensuous, apperceptive, and empathic response to pattern. [8a-b, d]

(c) Mood distribution rests on the patterned interplay of lyric and dramatic emphases, through mood definition and mood diversification.

   1. Mood definition (lyric)
     a. Initiation
     b. Prolongation
     c. Intensification
     d. Diffusion in the comprehensive mood pattern
   2. Mood diversification
     a. Immediate mood contrast (dramatic)
     b. Evolving mood contrast (lyrico-dramatic)

(d) In the distribution of mood, progression is cumulative and shapes the comprehensive mood pattern.

(e) Mood distribution and the course of the aesthetic pace are collateral.

(f) The comprehensive pattern of mood distribution largely determines the prevailing aesthetic temperament [3d], since the component characteristic moods tend to reflect the temperament congenial to them.

[5c(11) *Style distribution*

¶1 Style distribution concerns the character of, succession of, and emphasis among, the spans of style, within the general style homogeneity of the work as a whole. [5c(11g)]

(a) The character of style is in part preconceived by the composer, in part shaped concurrently with his evolution of the pattern.

(b) Style distribution rests on the patterned interplay of style contrasts, through style definition and style diversification.

    1. Style definition

        a. Initiation

        b. Prolongation

        c. Intensification

        d. Diffusion in the comprehensive style pattern

[5c(11b)] *2.* Style diversification

        a. Immediate style contrast (associated with rhetorical or dramatic emphasis)

        b. Evolving style contrast

(c) Distribution of style contrasts

    1. Range of style contrast: Wide . . . Narrow

    2. Style contrast is controlled in the interests of an essential general homogeneity of style. [5c(11g)]

    3. Style contrast follows the course of pattern and mood.

(d) Style distribution is marked by progression toward relative complexity.

(e) Progression in the distribution of style is cumulative.

[5c(11)] (f) The comprehensive pattern of style distribution embraces all other pattern, shaping the component patterns and integrating them.

(g) Comprehensive style homogeneity

    1. At most a general homogeneity, or at least an effective compatibility, of styles within a comprehensive style pattern, is essential to aesthetic value.

    2. Differences in treatment; cf. [30k]

        a. A more consistent homogeneity of style attends, e.g.,

97

(1) The romantic lyric miniature (e.g., Schumann, *Mondnacht,* op. 39, no. 5 (*Liederkreis*))

(2) The expansive classic work (e.g., Mozart, Symphony, K. 551, C maj., "Jupiter")

b. A less consistent homogeneity of style attends, e.g.,

(1) The expansive romantic work (e.g., Schumann, Phantasie, C maj., op. 17, pianoforte)

(2) The discursive realistic or dramatic work (e.g., Berlioz, *Harold en Italie,* G maj., op. 16; R. Strauss, *Salome*)

A. *Style from the Viewpoint of Pattern* (*continued*)

6. PARTICULAR INFLUENCES BEARING ON THE FORMULATION OF PATTERN

a. Influence *from the individual composer*

(1) His inheritance

(a) General historical heritage

(b) Direct influence from preceding or contemporary composers

(2) His environment; cf. [27a-h, m]

(3) His artistic personality

(a) His aesthetic temperament [3d; 24]

(b) His chosen degree of emphasis between the sensuous and intellectual impacts of pattern [8]

(c) His artistic creed [25]

(d) His originality

¶1 Arresting qualities, distinctive individuality, character, personality, are marks of style originality.

¶2 The quality of originality manifested in pattern and expressive effect imparts final, unique identity to the composer's art.

(e) His artistic integrity

¶1 The quality of sincerity communicated by the total style gives conviction to the composer's art.

98

[6 b. Influence of *extra-musical suggestion*

¶1 Observe that the intended function of a work will influence the character of pattern. [30j]

(1) Boundaries of extra-musical suggestion [9b(1b-2)]

(a) Musical pattern is somewhat adaptable to collaborating with extra-musical material, without loss of musical intelligibility or integrity.

[6b(1) (b) The conviction of such music rests chiefly on a *plausible correspondence* between the extra-musical stimulus and the expressive effect of the musical pattern.

(c) Degrees of correspondence

1. Delineation (generalization of the suggestion of the extra-musical source, e.g., Debussy, *Prélude à l'après-midi d'un faune*)

2. Description (an attempt to represent in the pattern literal particulars of the extra-musical source, within the delineative generalization, e.g., R. Strauss, *Don Quixote,* D maj., op. 35)

¶1 Literal depiction has limitations in the role which it can play in rational musical pattern and expressive effect. [9b(1b)IV]

(d) An authentic text, drama, program, ballet or pantomime plot, or a pictorial or sculptured representation, *specified by the composer,* becomes an intrinsic part of the total work of art.

(e) The extra-musical material may exert a preconditioning influence on the perceiver directly, as well as in collaboration with the musical pattern.

[6b   (2) The chief extra-musical influences

¶1 Observe that the intended function of a work will condition the character of pattern. [30j]

(a) *Text* (in vocal music)

¶1 Musical pattern is concurrent with the text.

¶2 The following musical factors may be influenced in greater or lesser degree by the text:

99

1. Pace

    a. Temporal pace

    b. Aesthetic pace

¶1 The pace of language is inherently faster than the structural and expressive pace of music.

2. Melody/rhythm, with respect to—

    a. Pitch range

    b. Pitch contour (influence of language)

      (1) Inflection

      (2) Tensity (consonance-dissonance)

      (3) Rhetorical emphasis

      (4) Phraseology

      (5) Delineative or descriptive detail

    c. Rhythmic pattern (influence of language)

      (1) Accentuation

      (2) Language rhythm

       (a) Stylized

       (b) Speechlike

    d. Determination of structural cadences

      (1) Location

      (2) Weight

[6b(2a)]   *3.* Harmony/rhythm, with respect to—

    a. Tensity pattern

    b. Choice of harmonic progression

    c. Chord-stream color

    d. Delineative or descriptive detail

4. Structure/rhythm, with respect to—

    a. Thematic pattern

    b. Structural rhythm

    c. Phraseology

    d. Proportion

      (1) Symmetrical

      (2) Asymmetrical

    e. Climax pattern

    f. Approximate form

(1) Adoption of the textual form

(2) Maintenance of the musical form, requiring the repetition of phrases, etc., of the text

g. The larger form, surrounding the text, which may include instrumental introductions, interludes, and postludes

[6b(2a)]   *5.* Dynamics, with respect to—
   a. Special dynamic emphases
   b. General dynamic level
   c. Dynamic contrasts

   6. Tone color or timbre, with respect to—
   a. Color nuance
   b. General color quality

   7. Idiom; see [3c(1-3)]

   8. Aesthetic pace, with respect to—
   a. Tensive pattern
   b. Progression pattern
   c. Delineative climax pattern

   9. Mood, follows the text in—
   a. Individual moods
      (1) Lyric
      (2) Dramatic
      (3) Lyrico-dramatic
   b. Mood progression
   c. Comprehensive mood

   10. Style, follows the text in—
   a. Local style detail
   b. Style contrast
   c. Style progression
   d. Comprehensive style

[6b(2)]   (b) *Drama* (in opera, music drama, dramatic oratorio, etc.)

¶1 Musical pattern is concurrent with the drama.

¶2 The following musical factors are influenced by the text and dramatic situation:

101

[6b(2b)]   *1.* Pace, as in [6b(2a)*1*]

                 2. Melody/rhythm, as in [6b(2a)*2*]

                 3. Melodic differentiations

                    a. Solo and dialogue passages

                       (1) Recitative

                         (a) Stylized speech
                         (b) Speechlike

                       (2) Formal melody

                       (3) Declamatory melody, largely of motive or thematic quality (arioso, Wagnerian melos, etc.)

                    b. Ensemble and choral passages

                       (1) Formal melody in set pieces
                       (2) Flexible melody in passages of realistic participation in the action

                    c. Orchestral passages

                       (1) Formal melody
                       (2) Flexible melody

                 4. Characteristic thematic material (motives, themes), as in [6b(2a)*2*]; also—

                    a. Delineative pitch detail
                    b. Delineative or descriptive pitch detail
                    c. Delineative or descriptive rhythmic detail
                    d. Delineative or descriptive harmonic detail

                 5. Harmony/rhythm, as in [6b(2a)*3*]

[6b(2b)]   *6.* Structure/rhythm, as in [6b(2a)*4*]; also—

                    a. Adaptation to the scene-act structure of the drama

                    b. The thematic material deployed according to the drama

                    c. Divisions follow those of the dramatic text

                       (1) Sectionally
                       (2) Continuously
                       (c) Mixed

    d. Forms

       (1) Conventional or adapted

       (2) Through-developed structure

       (3) Combination

       (4) Formal set pieces (numbers)

       (5) Flexible passages in direct participation in the action

       (6) Extensive instrumental passages containing vocal passages within the larger form

  7. Dynamics, as in [6b(2a)*5*]

  8. Tone color or timbre, as in [6b(2a)*6*]

  9.· Musical ingredients reflecting the dramatic text

    a. Solo

    b. Dialogue

    c. Ensemble

    d. Choral

    e. Orchestral

  10. Musical treatment of the drama

    a. Formal

    b. Realistic

    c. Intermediate

  11. Idiom, see [3c(1-2)]

[6b(2b)] *12.* Aesthetic pace, as in [6b(2a)*9*]; also—

    a. Aesthetic pace of extensive units (scene, act, entire work)

    b. Wide range of pace from lyric to dramatic

  13. Mood follows the drama, as in [6b(2a)*9*]; also—

    a. Interpretation of dramatic situations

    b. Characterization

    c. The extensive mood pattern

  14. Style follows the drama, as in [6b(2a)*10*]

[6b(2)] (c) *Program* (in instrumental music)

¶1 Musical pattern is not precisely concurrent with the program.

A. The general order of the musical passages follows that of the corresponding passages in the program.

B. The extent of the musical passages may not coincide with that suggested by the corresponding passages in the program.

c. The extent is likely to be determined by the content of the program, by the emphasis desired by the composer, and by the musical time required to create that emphasis (e.g., lyric treatment requires prolonged proportionate time).

¶2 The following musical factors are influenced by the program:

1. Pace
   a. Temporal pace
   b. Aesthetic pace
2. Characteristic thematic material (motives, themes), as in [6b(2a)2; 6b(2b)4]
3. Harmony/rhythm, as in [6b(2a)3]
4. Structure/rhythm, as in [6b(2a)4a-e]
5. Dynamics, as in [6b(2a)5]
6. Tone color or timbre, as in [6b(2a)6]
7. Idiom, see [3c(1-3)]
8. Aesthetic pace, as in [6b(2a)8]
9. Mood, as in [6b(2a)9]; also—
   a. Interpretations of program situations
   b. The extensive mood pattern
10. Style, as in [6b(2a)10]

[6b(2)   (d) *Plot* (in ballet or pantomime)

¶1 Plot influences musical pattern in a way similar to the influence of a program [6b(2c)]; also in—

1. The added stimulus of interpretative action
2. The prominence of rhythmic characteristics

(e) *Title* (in instrumental music)

¶1 Title, without program, influences musical pattern in a

way similar to, but less specific than, the influence of a program, as in [6b(2c)]; also—

   1. Details, if any, are supplied somewhat arbitrarily by the connotations of the title.

   2. The composer may supply an explanatory subtitle or verse motto.

   3. The performer or perceiver may intrude his own interpretative suggestion.

[6b(2)]   (f) *Title of a representation,* such as a picture, sculpture, etc., or a scene in nature, (in instrumental music)

¶1 These influence musical pattern in a way similar to, but less specific than, the influence of a program. [6b(2c)]; also—

   1. An added interpretation may come from the accepted meaning of the representation.

   2. Further interpretation may be introduced by the imagination of the performer or perceiver.

B. *Style from the Viewpoint of Expressive Effect*

7. THE SOURCE OF EXPRESSIVE EFFECT

   a. The *potential of characteristic expressive effect* is immanent in pattern.

   b. The pattern of tones in motion, reaching the perceiver from the composer through the intervention of performance, produces a complex though unified response on the part of the perceiver. This is the *expressive effect* of the work, or, less precisely, the "expression." [2b]

¶1 Distinguish from the vague notion of "expression" as mere emotional emphasis.

   c. The *perceiver's experience* constitutes the expressive effect.

8. THE ASPECTS OF THE PERCEIVER'S EXPERIENCE

¶1 Although the experience itself is indivisible, it is reasonable to inspect its aspects separately.

a. The *sensuous aspect*

    (1) Sensations of motion

        (a) Temporal pace

            1. Rate of motion

            2. Beat pulsation

            3. Fluctuation of pace

            4. Contrasts of pace

        (b) Fluctuating dynamics

        (c) Fluctuating tensities

            1. Tensities of melodic motion

            2. Tensities of consonance-dissonance

            3. Tensities of harmonic motion

            4. Tensities of structural motion

            5. Tensities of emerging, culminating, and resolving climax

        (d) Fluctuating mass

        (e) Fluctuating textural complexity

        (f) Momentum of the patterned motion embodied in progression [5c(6e)]

[8a   (2) Sensations of color

        (a) Organic color (consonance-dissonance)

            1. Individual colors

            2. The stream of color

        (b) Tone color or timbre

            1. Instruments

            2. Voices

            3. Other sounds

            4. Mixtures

[8 b. The *apperceptive aspect*

    (1) Concurrent following of the activities of pattern by the perceiver (in part, spontaneously analytical)

(a) Comparison [5b(1)]

(b) Expectation [5b(2)]

[8b   (2) Concurrent reconstruction of the pattern by the perceiver

(3) The accumulation of the pattern by the perceiver

(4) Final synthesis of the pattern by the perceiver [8h]

c. Varying *emphases between the sensuous and appercep-tive aspects* in the experience of different perceivers [18b (1)]

d. The *empathic aspect* of the experience

¶1 Empathy is the attribution of expressive effects to particular corresponding factors in the pattern which stimulate them.

(1) Empathic response attributed to the sensuous stimuli of the pattern [8a]

(2) Empathic response attributed to the apperceptive stimuli of the pattern [8b]

(3) Empathic response attributed to the specialized delineative or descriptive activities of the pattern [9b(1b)]

(4) Synthesis of empathic responses

[8   e. The *mood quality* of the experience

¶1 The moods of music, experienced as they are in detachment [8f], are not the emotions of reality, but are rather an aspect of the aesthetic emotion.[18]

¶2 Mood in the perceiver's experience is empathically influenced.

¶3 While moods arise basically from the stimulus of pattern, they are colored and amplified by the perceiver's imagination, which they stimulate as they evolve.

(1) Saturation with mood

(2) Range of mood quality: Assertive mood . . . Vague mood

(3) Variety of mood

[18] An older term which the author wishes to preserve. See Ethel D. Puffer, *op. cit.*, pp. 196-201.

(4) Definition of mood; Intense . . . Detense

(5) Background mood across which other, usually related, moods play

[8e (7) The chief and more tangible moods of music

    (a) Names given to moods are imprecise suggestions of the actual moods experienced.

    (b) Types of mood

        1. Some suggested scales of basic moods

            a. Tranquil, gentle, pastoral, genial

            b. Energetic, animated, agitated, bold, imposing, bombastic, aggressive

            c. Impersonal, serene, intimate, introspective

            d. Sentimental, tender, pathetic, passionate

            e. Sober, dignified, noble, majestic, heroic, tragic, desperate

            f. Sombre, mysterious, sinister, ominous

            g. Pleasant, cheerful, gay, boisterous, frenzied

            h. Whimsical, humorous, comic, satirical, ironical

[8e(7b) *2.* Moods felt as mixtures, e.g.,

            a. Whimsical + pathetic = wistful

            b. Energetic + pathetic = heroic

            c. Tranquil + pathetic = sentimental
            etc.

        3. Other intermediate moods and blends

¶1 Certain moods associated with music, such as patriotic, military, religious, erotic, etc., tend to involve for their definition the aid of title, text, or other association, or the special predisposition of the perceiver.

(8) Mood pattern, involving—

    (a) Related moods

    (b) Contrasting moods

    (c) Evolving succession of moods

    (d) Overlapping moods

    (e) Aesthetic pace as the index of mood pattern

[8 f. *Detachment* of the experience
    (1) Personal disinterestedness
    (2) Freedom from drives
    (3) Psychical distance[19]

  g. The *amplitude* of the experience
    (1) Concurrent with the response to pattern
      (a) Affective response
      (b) Apperceptive response
    (2) Immediate retrospective synthesis on completion of the pattern [8h]
    (3) Partly concurrent, partly delayed
      (a) Appreciative response
      (b) Evaluative response [42f]

[8 h. *Retrospective synthesis* of the experience
    (1) The temporal dispersion of music necessitates, on the part of the perceiver, an ultimate synthesis of the pattern and expressive effect in a single, though complex, impression. Details of style, discovered by analysis, fuse into a total, mature, individualized impression of a work—its identity. Analysis is absorbed and disappears.
    (2) This reflective synthesis in repose contributes an aesthetically gratifying resolution of the tensities accumulated in following the pattern.
    (3) Music reviewed in the imagination is free from the literal application of time controls. [5a(4b)]
    (4) Collateral with the perceiver's re-creation of the pattern, a broadly lyric accumulation of mood takes place, which results in an increasingly defined general mood—the issue of the pattern and an intrinsic part of the expressive effect. This comprehensive *lyric frame* assimilates the variety of changing moods and is an aspect of the larger homogeneity of style essential to aesthetic value. [5c(11g)*1*]

[19] See Edward Bullough, "Psychical Distance," in *British Journal of Psychology*, vol. 5, 1912, pp. 87-118.

[8 j. The *perceiver's pleasure* (aspects of a single pleasure)

(1) Sensuous pleasure in the play of motion and color in sound

(2) Intellectual pleasure in following and reconstructing the logic of pattern

(3) Pleasure in the stimulation of the perceiver's aesthetic faculty

(4) Pleasure in identification with the creative and poetic vitality of the work

(5) Pleasure in the artistic integrity of the work

k. The essence of a fine work of musical art during its course invades and pervades the personality of the perceiver.

9. EXPRESSIVE EFFECT AS COMMUNICATION

a. The *nature* of musical communication

(1) Contact between the composer and the perceiver is incomplete because of the vagaries of notation and performance. [13-14, 15]

(2) Contact between the composer and the perceiver may be further impaired because of interpositions on the part of the perceiver in his response to pattern [18], e.g.,

(a) Substitutions
(b) Subtractions
(c) Irrelevant additions
(d) Unawareness
(e) Insensitiveness
(f) Antipathy

[9a (3) Communication from the composer to the perceiver is limited to whatever is common to the pattern of the composer and the direct response of the perceiver to the pattern. The whole of the composer's available stimulation from the pattern is not always operative in eliciting the perceiver's response.

(4) The net communication from the composer to the

perceiver consists in the perceiver's consciousness of, sensitiveness to, and pleasure in, the state into which the aesthetic experience, derived directly from the pattern, has put him. [8]

¶1 Distinguish between the communication of intrinsic meaning [9b(1a)], i.e., the musical experience *per se,* and the communication of extrinsic meaning [9b(1b)], i.e., the musical experience entangled with something non-musical.

(5) Beyond the boundary of direct response to pattern and beyond the resultant communication transmitted, the imagination of the perceiver (cf. "optimum perceiver" [2b(5), 18d]) may contribute a relevant increment of personal and individual origin, beyond the capacity of musical communication, in consummation of the ultimate aesthetic experience. [8h]

¶1 Observe that music as a medium of communication is not identical with music as manifested in the ultimate aesthetic experience.

[9   b. The *meaning* of the communication[20]

(1) The range of meaning

¶1 The following categories overlap and merge, suggesting a continuous graduation from general to specific meaning:

(a) Intrinsic meaning

i. General meaning

1. Aesthetic pleasure in pattern *per se*

2. Enhancement of the pleasure through its stimulation of a concurrent mood experience [8e]

¶1 This is the primary and essential meaning of music.

ii. General meaning heightened

3. Suggestion of further definition of meaning through empathic responses (e.g., rising, falling, etc.) [8d]

4. Suggestion of further definition of meaning

[20] See Glen Haydon, *On the Meaning of Music,* Washington, D.C., Library of Congress, 1948.

through individual, personal associations (on the margin of extrinsic meaning)

[9b(1)] (b) Extrinsic meaning

¶1 Extrinsic meaning is *attributed* meaning through reference to extra-musical sources.

¶2 These sources supply the specificness furnished only by the collaboration of linguistic or visual media; they are external to the unique intrinsic meaning of pattern itself.

¶3 *Plausible correspondence* between aspects of the pattern and the extra-musical source is sufficient to give some conviction to their association. [6b(1b)]

¶4 Extra-musical suggestion in text, program, title, etc., may, and is intended to, condition the perceiver during or in advance of his hearing of the musical work, with consequent effect on the experience.

[9b(1b)] ¶5 Extra-musical suggestion tends to enlarge the range of expressive effects undertaken in music and more closely to define them.

¶6 The boundaries of extrinsic meaning:

A. Extrinsic meaning, unless offered by the composer himself as an inherent part of his concept of the total artistic work, is arbitrary, may be irrelevant, and is inessential.

B. Extrinsic meaning is not aesthetically valid unless it is submersible in and carried by intrinsic meaning.

C. Extrinsic meaning may frequently appear as a momentary and incidental heightening of intrinsic meaning.

III. Specific meaning approached

5. Definition of meaning through inferences of meaning drawn from the extra-musical source (e.g., from the title or general program) [6b(1c)*1*]

6. Definition of meaning through recognizable conventions of meaning (e.g., military trumpet call)

7. Sustained *delineation* of extra-musical meaning, often implemented by the re-use and development of characteristic musical ideas manipulated in part

according to the dictates of the extra-musical source (e.g., the *Leitmotiv*)

iv. Specific meaning

8. Descriptive *representation* of specific extra-musical meaning [6b(1c)*2*]

   a. Approximate realistic depiction keyed to and supported by the extra-musical source (e.g., a storm)

   b. Literal, self-explanatory imitation of an extra-musical source (e.g., cuckoo call)

¶1 The limitations of the resources of specific meaning are self-evident. Passages of descriptive representation are likely to be comparatively brief.

[9b] (2) Effect on pattern of the attempt to increase specificness of meaning

   (a) The absolute integrity of pattern *per se* is qualified in proportion to the increased specificness.

   (b) Pattern, however, is able to inflect in favor of specific meaning to a considerable extent without marked impairment of its logic and aesthetic value.

(3) Resources of pattern in support of meaning; see [6b(2)]

C. *Pattern* Cum *Expressive Effect as Design*

10. PATTERN AND EXPRESSIVE EFFECT

a. These two interdependent and inseparable complementary phases of style become one in the *style identity* of the work [2a-b]

b. Style identity is given its quality through the comprehensive *design* pervading the integral work; see TERMS, p. xi; [2c]

11. DESIGN

a. The integral work is a projection of the composer's *design concept*.

b. But the composer's concept is only partially foreseen by him and emerges in full concurrently as the pattern is created.

c. The design concept of the work—its creative source—arises and is nourished as an *idealization* in the imagination of the composer.

d. Design realized becomes a unique achievement of the creative artistic spirit.

III. The Contingency of Style on Notation, Performance, and the Perceiver

12. THE ROLE OF NOTATION, PERFORMANCE, AND THE PERCEIVER

a. Notation provides an approximate record, varying in precision, of the composer's musical pattern.

b. Performance assumes the obligation of inferring and interpreting the composer's intent from the notated record, imparting to the musical work auditory reality and palpable style identity.

c. Performance is hence subject to the terms of notation, and style to those of performance, while the perceiver is in turn, to a certain extent, circumscribed by the style interpretation offered by performance, and by his own capacity.

A. The Device of Notation

13. THE VARIABILITY OF NOTATION

a. Notation varies in form, method, and precision, in different epochs, localities, and types of music.

b. The facilities of notation tend, in general, to fall behind or remain inadequate to the requirements of the music and composer.

14. THE LIMITATIONS OF NOTATION

a. A precise written record of musical pattern, an ideal desirable in itself, is nevertheless likely to be space-consuming and limited in application.

b. Practical notation is content to resort to various approximations.

c. An approximate written notation has the advantage over an exact sound-recording, valuable for its reality, in offering to composer, performer, and critic, facility in the immediate comparison of successive or separated components of the pattern. [16f]

d. In modern notation, discrepancies exist between notation according to the inherited concept of the circle of fifths (up and down) and notation according to equal temperament. This situation may affect the precision of the notation.

e. In most notation, verbal indications, special symbols, and conventionalized understandings, all more or less imprecise, are relied upon to supplement or clarify the basic notation.

f. Full knowledge of the implications of any notation is essential to performance.

[14 g. The limitations of conventional notation may be bypassed by the composer's designating the exact pitch, time, dynamic, and timbre relations in terms of electronic reproduction.

B. *The Contribution of Performance*

15. THE QUALIFICATION OF NOTATION IN PERFORMANCE

a. Interpretative deviations from and additions to the literal basic notation of the pattern are essential to significant performance.

b. Such deviations constitute inflections of the notated

pattern and impart flexible molding to the melodic, textural, harmonic, and structural members.

c. These inflections, rendered in performance, become intrinsic to the pattern of the audibly revealed style.

d. Types of pattern inflection in performance (lacking or imperfectly shown in the notation)

 (1) Pitch inflection of the pattern

  (a) Vibrato

  (b) Adaptive intonation (e.g., raised or lowered pitch for rising or falling chromatic tones; adaptation of pitch for purity of intonation, as in string quartet and choral performance, etc.)

   1. Melodic

   2. Harmonic

  (c) Pitch generalization (e.g., *Sprechstimme*)

  (d) Portamento, glissando

[15d (2) Rhythmic inflection of the pattern

  (a) Agogics

  (b) Locally inflected rubato

  (c) Structural rubato [5c(3d)4]

  (d) Speechlike pliability (chiefly in vocal music, but cf. instrumental recitative)

 (3) Dynamic inflection of the pattern

  (a) Dynamic accent, as an agent in rhythmic definition

  (b) Rhetorical emphasis, as an agent in melodic/rhythmic and structural/rhythmic definition

  (c) Dynamic nuance, as an agent in shaping the structure

[15d(3) (d) Varied fluctuating dynamic nuances, as an agent in the molding of expressive effect

  (e) Interlinear dynamic adjustment, as an agent in securing textural perspective [4b(4c)2]

  (f) Adjustment of relative dynamic levels as bases of reference

(4) Tone color or timbre characterization of the pattern

(a) This is not often indicated verbally in the notation (but cf. the occasionally specified timbres of different registers and colors of voices and instruments).

(b) Relation to dynamics: tone color or timbre undergoes change with dynamic and pitch change.

[15 e. Determination of tempo in performance

(1) Tempo approaching that intended by the composer will be sought by the interpreter.

(2) Tempo is at least suggested in the nature of the pattern and its rhythmic activities, and sometimes by the character of the notation.

(3) Determination of tempo is an interpretative prerogative, and significantly affects the character of the pattern and its expressive effect.

(4) Tempo and tempo change may be broadly indicated by the composer through the use of conventional terms.

(5) In much music from the time of Maelzel, metronome numbers give a close indication of the composer's (or editor's) intention, but are not narrowly binding on the performer.

(6) Rhythmic inflections take place within the basic tempo.

f. Supplementation of the notation in performance

(1) Realization of abbreviated ornamentation

(2) Realization of the *basso continuo* [3c(1c)*3*; 4b(5a); 4b(7)¶2]

(3) Added improvised ornamentation (e.g., in baroque practice)

(4) Improvisation of the cadenza

16. THE ART OF INTERPRETATIVE PERFORMANCE

a. The performer as an intermediary and participant

(1) The obligation of the performer to the composer

(2) The discretion of the performer as an artist

(3) Stylistic imagination on the part of the performer

(4) The re-creative contribution of the performer

[16 b. Re-creation of the notated pattern in performance

(1) Realization of the progressing logic of the pattern

(2) Realization of the integrity of the structural pattern in the large

(3) Infusion of flexibility into the notated pattern

(4) Realization of the implied aesthetic pace in the interests of expressive effect

(5) Evocation of the implied mood pattern

(6) Fulfillment of the total style

c. Different temperaments in performance

(1) Counterparts of the aesthetic temperaments underlying pattern [3d]

(a) Classic temperament

(b) Romantic temperament

(c) Eclecticism

(2) Consequences of friction between the intrinsic temperament of the musical work and the innate temperament of the performer, e.g.,

(a) The romantic interpretation of classic styles

(b) The classic interpretation of romantic styles

(c) Other anomalous mixtures

[16 d. Different conceptions of the role of performance

(1) Restoration

(a) Founded upon an historical basis

(b) Rendering according to the principles and taste of the epoch which produced the work

(c) Addressed primarily to the connoisseur

(2) Stylization

(a) Reappraisal and translation, according to the predilections of the performer, of the principles and taste of the epoch which produced the work

(b) A doctrinaire approach

[16d(2) (c) Rendering historically neutral
        (d) Addressed to the popular audience
[16d (3) Idealization
        (a) A vision of the work
        (b) The performer tends to equal the composer
        (c) Rendering varies with the temperaments and enthusiasms of performer and perceiver
        (d) Addressed primarily to the intensively intuitive perceiver
      (4) Contemporization
        (a) An iconoclastic appropriation of the work
        (b) Transfer of the work to the present, its own past context largely ignored or suppressed
        (c) Imposition of contemporary technical and expressive concepts
        (d) Addressed primarily to the appropriate cult
[16d (5) Eclectic combinations of ingredients from more than one of the above conceptions of performance
        (a) Conflicts
        (b) Reconciliations
        (c) Hybrids
      (6) The performance practices of different epochs and styles (for the restoration of the musical work)
      (7) The personal element in any conception of performance
[16 e. The status of technique in performance
      (1) A controlled or subordinated tool of interpretation
      (2) A vehicle of virtuosic display
      (3) Intermediates
      (4) Effect on style of the attitude of the performer toward technique
[16 f. Silent reading of notation
      (1) A subjective substitute for performance
      (2) The sensuous responses to actual sound are at-

tenuated or largely lacking, though an experienced reader can supply much.

(3) Comparisons are facilitated

(4) Partial and convenient condensation of time is secured.

17. THE MEDIA OF PERFORMANCE

a. Style as derived from the medium

(1) Music composed for the individual medium is characterized by stylistic detail and by a general style conceived according to the nature, requirements, and resources of the medium.

(2) Some works are composed so as to permit choice between or from among different media; such styles are neutral or are compromises.

(3) Only a limited amount of music is composed in the abstract, without reference to a specified or understood medium, (e.g., Bach, *Die Kunst der Fuge*).

(4) The style of the medium is an aspect of and intrinsic part of the general style of a work, (e.g., piano style, choral style, etc.).

(a) Congeniality in the treatments of pattern and medium

(b) Discrepancies in the treatments of pattern and medium

[17 b. The effects of the medium on style

¶1 The character and treatment of the medium bear upon all of the components of pattern in one degree or another.

(1) The effect of the mechanism and manner of tone production

(2) The effect of the technique of the medium

(3) The effect of the sustaining power

(4) The effect of agility afforded (to a certain extent related to the size and pitch of the medium)

(5) The effect of the sonority

(6) The effect of the timbre

(a) Variability of timbre within the individual medium, according to—

1. Register

2. Pitch level

3. Dynamic level

4. Tone production

[17b(6) (b) Individualization of melodic pattern by timbre

(c) Application of timbre to textural/harmonic differentiations

(d) Composite timbre

1. Blends and contrasts of two or more media

2. The components are balanced both by the orchestration itself and by the performers.

(7) In music with text, the effect of language and its meaning on the style of the medium (as well as on the total pattern) [6b(2a)]

[17 c. The particular grouping of instruments, voices, or instruments and voices, is a partial determinant of style and is inherent in the style of the ensemble, (e.g., string quartet, accompanied song, etc.). [32e, i-ii, 37, 75]

d. Classification of the media

¶1 Extensive classification of the media and consideration of their styles lie beyond the scope of this *Handbook.*[21, 22, 23]

(1) Solo

(a) Instrument

(b) Voice

(2) Ensemble

(a) Instruments

1. Solo combinations

2. The larger combinations

[21] For extensive classification and description of the media, see books on keyboard instruments and on instrumentation and orchestration; see also Willi Apel, *op. cit.*, pp. 355-357.

[22] For the history of instruments, see Curt Sachs, *The History of Musical Instruments*, New York, 1940; Karl Geiringer, *The History of Musical Instruments*, London, 1943.

[23] For consideration of the aspect of style which stems specifically from the nature of the medium, see works on the individual media.

(b) Voices
  1. Solo combinations
  2. The larger combinations
(c) Instruments and voices

C. The Variable Perceiver

18. THE PERCEIVER IN THE COMPOSER-NOTATION-PERFORMER-PERCEIVER SEQUENCE

a. The final imprint of style resides in the imagination of the perceiver.

b. The qualifications of the perceiver are variable. They are subject to training.

[18b (1) Native predilections

  (a) Attraction by the sensuous aspect of the musical experience

  (b) Attraction by the intellectual and apperceptive aspect of the musical experience

  (c) Attraction by the extra-musical basis of the work, if any

  (4) The importance to the perceiver of attempting to balance these aspects in an aesthetically significant proportion

  (2) Sensitivity

  (a) Perception of pitch and its relations
  (b) Response to rhythm and its relations
  (c) Response to color and its relations
  (d) Intuitive-artistic perceptiveness
  (e) Receptiveness to the aesthetic temperaments [3d]

[18b (3) Power of attention

  (a) Vividness of attention
  (b) Uniform sustainment of attention
  (c) Span of attention
  (d) Power of selective attention

(4) Attitude

(a) Indulgence in prejudices in favor of or against various aspects of a work, composer, or style, derived from—

1. Preferences based on aesthetic temperament

2. Arbitrary personal predilections (sometimes traceable to personal inadequacy)

(b) Catholicity

[18b   (5) Individual associations

(a) General (racial, cultural, religious, etc.)
(b) Personal

(6) Accumulated experience

(7) Background of knowledge

(a) The historical and cultural background of the work

(b) The composer's artistic personality

(c) Any designated functional purpose of the work

[18b   (8) Imagination

(9) Taste (a product of education through the exercise of criticism)

(10) Intellectual power of analysis-synthesis

[18 c. The perceiver's interventions in the composer's and performer's presentations, usually unconscious, involve [9a(2)]—

(1) Substitutions
(2) Subtractions
(3) Irrelevant additions
(4) Unawareness
(5) Insensitiveness
(6) Antipathy

d. Hypothecation of the "optimum perceiver" is necessitated, as an ideal in the approximate reconciliation of the composer's and perceiver's concepts. [2b(5)]

D. The Relativity of Style

19. THE VARIABILITY OF STYLE AS HEARD

a. Constantly varying renderings of the style of a work are inevitable.

b. Traditions of performance persist.

c. Fashions in performance fluctuate and at times dominate.

d. The notated basis of pattern nevertheless remains intact for further interpretations (except as editors tamper with the pattern, or transcription misrepresents the original style, or problems in transcribing the notation intrude).

20. THE DURABILITY OF STYLE

a. Style acknowledges an obligation to performance but at the same time transcends it in durability and essential integrity.

b. Style enjoys a prolonged existence, beyond the conceptions of the individual performer and perceiver, in the collective impress on a given time or generation.

c. Style may also acquire a cumulative existence over as long a time as the historical-cultural context remains the same or similar.

d. A past, even remote, style may at a later time acquire a contemporary conviction in an epoch in which a reversion to, or restoration of, or reminiscence of, the principles of the earlier style is cultivated, (e.g., contemporary baroque).

e. Beyond that, the perpetuation or resuscitation of authentic style is dependent on the scholarship, historical imagination, and aesthetic insight, of historians [33-36], of style critics [38-43], and of performers [15-16].

IV. The Historical Context of Style

21. THE HISTORICAL BASIS OF STYLE

a. Style is the product of the intersection of time, place, and creative temperament, working within the frame of the nature of the art. [1c]

b. The foundations of style, which endure throughout change, are—

(1) The essentially constant nature of pattern

(2) The essentially constant nature of expressive effect

c. Their applications, however, are subject to the continual change of historical circumstance.

d. The exercise of scholarship and historical imagination is essential in the historical approach to style.

A. *The Style Epoch*

22. DELINEATION OF THE EPOCH

a. An epoch is an historical span marked by significantly related phenomena, rather than by fixed time limits.

b. An epoch is signalized by the appearance, gradual or rapid, of a new viewpoint, characterized by substantially new manifestations or fresh applications in the technical processes of pattern and in the expressive potential.

c. In spite of divergencies among the component styles of an epoch [23], significant common factors of pattern and expressive effect prevail.

d. The epoch is not necessarily motivated by a single aesthetic temperament, though one is likely to be predominant; (cf. e.g., the romantic period).

e. A defining individuality, characteristic of the epoch as a whole, is evident.

f. Epochs overlap, even though well defined.

g. The style epochs of music correspond nominally with those of the other arts.

23. DIFFERENT PHASES OF THE EPOCH

a. Chronologically different phases are marked by similar phenomena appearing at different times within the epoch.

b. Geographically different phases are marked by similar phenomena appearing at different places within the epoch, at the same time, or at different times.

c. Temperamentally different phases are usually marked by common ground in pattern and technical processes.

[23 d. Minority phenomena stimulate diversity from and conflict with the prevailing traits of the epoch, while not vitiating the essential viewpoint of the epoch. Splinter styles, secondary styles, and even partially dissenting styles occur.

e. A larger and prevailing integrity of style tends to unite the phases of the epoch.

24. THE AESTHETIC TEMPERAMENTS AS MOTIVATIONS OF THE EPOCH OR SUBDIVISION

¶1 See [3d]
a. Classic temperament
b. Romantic temperament
c. Eclecticism
   (1) Reconciliation of temperaments
   (2) Conflict of temperaments
   (3) Blends of temperament

25. DIFFERENT ARTISTIC CREEDS AS MOTIVATIONS OF THE EPOCH OR SUBDIVISION

a. Orthodox creed
b. Progressive creed

c. Iconoclastic creed

d. Eclecticism

26. SUBDIVISION OF THE EPOCH

a. The subdivisions are subject individually to the same delimitations [22], phases [23], temperamental motivations [24], and artistic creeds [25], as those of the epoch.

b. The hierarchy of the epoch and subdivision

    (1) Chronological

      (a) Epoch

      (b) Periods of the epoch

    (2) Geographical, ethnic

      (a) Region

      (b) Country, nation

      (c) Ethnic strain

[26b   (3) Collective

      (a) Movement (a tendency of major scope, e.g., the romantic movement)

      (b) School (a group of composers with similar artistic principles and practices, e.g., the Mannheim School)

      (c) Periods of the school

    (4) Individual

      (a) Composer

      (b) Periods of the composer

      (c) Individual works of the composer

B. Historical Style Change

27. INFLUENCES BEARING ON HISTORICAL STYLE CHANGE

¶1 The following influences may operate singly or in combination to bring about style change:

a. Folk

b. Cultural

c. Religious, ecclesiastical
d. Social
e. Political
f. Economic
g. Geographical
h. National, ethnic
j. Influence of aesthetic temperament
k. Influence of technical experimentation
m. Influence of the other arts

28. THE HISTORICAL PANORAMA OF STYLES

a. The succession of style epochs and their subdivisions[24]

(1) This succession is the nucleus of music history.

(2) The rationale of the succession of epochs will be viewed according to whatever theory of history one chooses to hold.[25]

[28a (3) Chronological overlaps and geographical dispersion occur among the epochs and subdivisions.

(4) The style epochs of Western music history may be designated in considerable condensation as follows (cf. related periodization in the history of the other arts) :[26]

¶1 No dates are assigned here to the epochs and subdivisions indicated; the histories of music should be consulted.

¶2 The names of a few composers are given to assist in marking the style epochs referred to.

[28a(4)   I. ANTIQUITY

II. MIDDLE AGES

A. *Early Middle Ages*

1. Rise of the monophonic style in the music of the Christian Church (plain chant)

B. *Romanesque*

1. Emergence of the concept of polyphony in the music of the Christian Church (organum)

[24] Cf. James S. Ackerman, *op. cit.*
[25] See Glen Haydon, *Introduction to Musicology*, New York, 1941, pp. 247-266.
[26] See Willi Apel, *op. cit.*, ''History of Music,'' pp. 335-339; also various histories of music.

c. *Gothic*

1. Polyphonic style of the Ars Antiqua (discant; Pérotin, Franco of Cologne)

2. Lyric monophonic styles of the age of chivalry (Troubadours, Trouvères, etc.)

3. Polyphonic style of the Ars Nova (Machaut, Landino)

[28a(4)   III. RENAISSANCE

1. Diversification of styles under humanistic influence (Dufay, Ockeghem, Josquin des Prez)

2. Growing distinctions between ecclesiastical and secular styles (frottola, villanella, madrigal)

3. Increasing divergence of instrumental from vocal styles and emergence of independent instrumental styles (organ, lute, ensemble, etc.)

4. Afterreflection of the renaissance in the mature *a cappella* style (Palestrina, Lassus)

5. Relaxation of polyphonic style under individualistic influence (Vittoria, Gesualdo, Morley)

6. Adaptation of polyphonic style to instruments (G. Gabrieli, Sweelinck)

7. Emergence of the concept of homophony (Luis Milan, Dowland, Byrd)

IV. MODERN

A. *Baroque*

1. Rise of the interpretative dramatic style (Monteverdi)

2. Rise of the semi-liturgic Protestant service (M. Praetorius, Schein, Schütz)

3. Emergence of the formal dramatic style (Carissimi, Cavalli, Cesti, A. Scarlatti)

4. Admixture of interpretative and formal dramatic styles (Lully, Purcell)

5. Development of Protestant concerted church music (Tunder, Weckmann, Buxtehude)

6. Development of independent instrumental styles (Frescobaldi, Froberger, Bassani)

7. Consummation of baroque styles (Corelli, Vivaldi, Handel, J. S. Bach)

B. *Rococo*

1. Mutation of the baroque into the rococo style (Couperin, D. Scarlatti)

2. Convergence of baroque and rococo elements toward the classic (C. P. E. Bach, J. C. Bach)

C. *Classic*

1. Reassertion of the interpretative dramatic ideal in classic context (Gluck)

2. Consummation of classic architectonics (Haydn, Mozart)

3. Intensification of the classic toward assertive individualism (Beethoven)

[28a(4)]   D. *Romantic*

1. Dramatic style under romantic influence; folk-national elements (Weber)

2. Lyric style under romantic influence; personal inflections (Schubert, Schumann, Chopin)

3. Preservation of the classic in romantic context (Mendelssohn)

4. Modification of dramatic conventions under romantic influence (Rossini, Meyerbeer)

5. Emergence of romantic realism in program music (Berlioz, Liszt)

6. Intensification of romantic realism in dramatic styles (Wagner, Verdi)

7. Reconciliation of classic architectonics with romantic individualism (Brahms)

8. Romantic folk-nationalism as a cult (Mussorgsky, Dvořák)

9. Culmination of romantic realism in dramatic and lyric styles (R. Strauss, Hugo Wolf, Puccini)

10. Decline and diffusion of the late romantic, with implications of neo-romanticism and neo-baroque (Skriabin, Mahler, Reger)

11. Impressionism and anti-romantic reaction (Debussy)

v. contemporary eclecticism

1. Eclectic reversions in style, with novel technical vocabularies

¶1 Composers suggested as representatives of the following styles may cultivate more than one of the styles noted:

a. Neo-romanticism, expressionism (Schönberg, A. Berg)

b. Sophisticated primitivism (Stravinsky)

c. Neo-classicism (Milhaud, Stravinsky)

d. Pseudo-classicism (Stravinsky)

e. Neo-baroque (Hindemith, Stravinsky)

f. Neo-nationalism (Bartók, Prokofieff)

g. Mixtures and splinter schools

¶1 Music, devised with the aid of electronic apparatus or in which there is selection by methods of chance, awaits the possible demonstration of tone systems and definable styles.

[28a (5) Developmental change within the style epoch

¶1 Even though one may well reject a general evolutionary theory of history, the presence of organic development within the epoch or movement is evident, and suggests the following stages:

(a) Presage
(b) Rise
(c) Development
(d) Culmination
(e) Continuation
(f) Decline
(g) Absorption
(h) Dissipation
(j) Residue

[28 b. Style transition

    (1) Style mixture as the result of historical change

    (2) Modification of style characteristics toward another style

    (3) Individuality and independent integrity of transitional styles

        (a) Such styles sometimes lack technical security.

        (b) Compensation may lie in their progressive or prophetic qualities.

[28 c. Cross-influences among styles

    (1) Style mixture as the result of borrowing

    (2) Hybrid styles and blends, (e.g., the romantic strain in the baroque, the baroque element in the contemporary)

    (3) Reversions in style, (e.g., 20th century baroque, classic)

        (a) Sometimes progressive

        (b) Sometimes regressive

        (c) Sometimes inert

        (d) Sometimes artificial

d. Each epoch and each subdivision is subject to description, characterization, and criticism of its style.

C. The Orders and Types of Style

29. HISTORICAL ORIGIN

a. Various orders and types of style arise under different historical circumstances and change with those circumstances. [31-32]

b. The orders and types, originating in and characteristic of one epoch, may continue in modified form into the next epoch, or may be resumed or reverted to in later epochs (e.g., modal style: an order; lyric style: a type). Some may have considerable historical range (e.g., suite: a type), or may even be universal (e.g., melodic style: an order).

30. THE CHIEF MARKS OF THE ORDERS AND TYPES OF STYLE

¶1 Distinctions marking the orders and types of style may be made as follows, according to—

a. Vocabulary [3b], (e.g., modal style)

b. Idiom [3c], (e.g., polyphonic style)

c. Aesthetic temperament [3d], (e.g., romantic style)

[30 d. Elements of pattern [4], (e.g., melodic style, cursive style)

e. Mood pattern [8e(8)] and expressive effect [7-9], (e.g., lyric style)

f. Extra-musical influence [6b; 9b; 30j], (e.g., ecclesiastical style)

g. Medium [17], (e.g., pianoforte style)

h. Historical epoch or subdivision [22-26], (e.g., Ars Nova style, baroque style)

[30 j. Function
    (1) Folk
    (2) Sacred
      (a) Liturgic
      (b) Non-liturgic
    (3) Secular
      (a) Work
      (b) Play
      (c) Domestic
      (d) Court
      (e) Social
      (f) Salon
      (g) Entertainment
      (h) Dance
      (j) National, patriotic
      (k) Military
      (m) Concert
      (n) Operatic
      (p) Theater
      (q) Cinema
      (r) Occasional

[30 k. Treatment
    (1) Different forms of treatment
        (a) Miniature treatment (lyric; e.g., the lyric, the character piece)
        (b) Expansive treatment (lyrico-dramatic; e.g., the symphony)
        (c) Discursive treatment (lyrico-dramatic; e.g., the opera, the program symphony)
        (d) Intermediates
    (2) Distinctions in treatment are based on a combination of various aspects of style
        (a) The nature of the internal structure
        (b) The character of the extent
[30k(2) (c) Mood concentration or distribution
           1. Lyric
           2. Dramatic
           3. Lyrico-dramatic
           4. Blends
        (d) Style concentration or dispersion [5c(11)]
        (e) Artistic ideal

31. THE ORDERS OF STYLE

a. The orders of style are general categories, differing from one another considerably in range and specificness (cf. e.g., modal style, melodic style, lyric style, operatic style, etc.). In some instances the term "style," although often thus used, may seem somewhat loose (e.g., secular style, eclectic style).

b. The orders of style may divide into sub-orders, may overlap, exist within one another, and are subject to various cross-references; in particular the orders are subject to historical subdivision.

c. The main style orders are given below; in the following examples, they are distinguished and grouped according to the chief marks of style: [30]

Examples of the Style Orders

[31c   (1)   Vocabulary [3b]

    (a) Modal style
    (b) Tonal style
    (c) Amodal (atonal) style
    (d) Diatonic style
    (e) Chromatic style

  (2) Idiom [3c]

    (a) Monophonic style
    (b) Polyphonic style
    (c) Semi-polyphonic style
    (d) Homophonic style
    (e) Semi-homophonic style

  (3) Aesthetic temperament [3d]

    (a) Classic style
    (b) Romantic style
    (c) Eclectic style

  (4) Elements of pattern [4]

    (a) Melodic style
    (b) Textural/harmonic style
    (c) Structural style

[31c   (5)   Mood pattern and expressive effect [5c(7g)2]

    (a) Lyric style
    (b) Dramatic style
    (c) Lyrico-dramatic style

  (6) Extra-musical influence [6b; 9b]

    (a) Delineative style
    (b) Descriptive style

[31c   (7)   Medium [17]

    (a) Instrumental style
      1. Style of each instrument
      2. Solo ensemble styles
      3. Orchestral styles
    (b) Vocal style
      1. Style of each voice-type
      2. Solo ensemble styles

3. Choral styles

    a. A cappella style

    b. Vocal-instrumental style, for chorus, with or without soloist(s), and instrumental accompaniment

  (8) Historical epoch and subdivision [28a(4)], e.g.,

    (a) Gothic style

    (b) Baroque style

    (c) Classic style ⎱
    (d) Romantic style ⎰ (in their historical connotation)

    (e) Contemporary style

    etc.

[31c (9) Function [30j] e.g.,

    (a) Folk style

    (b) Salon style

    (c) National style

    (d) Operatic style

    etc.

  (10) Treatment [30k]

    (a) Miniature style

    (b) Expansive style

    (c) Discursive style

32. THE TYPES OF STYLE

a. The types of style,[27] comprised within the more general orders of style, are specific *style practices,* distinguished by characteristic combinations of the marks of style. [30] Some of the types are popularly but inadvisedly spoken of as "forms," e.g., the opera "form," with consequent confusion with a more precise meaning of the term "form," SEE TERMS, p. XI

b. Distinctions of sub- or related types from a basic type lie chiefly along the following lines:

  (1) The same type in different historical epochs (e.g., the classic and romantic sonata)

---

[27] See Willi Apel, *op. cit.,* "History of Music," especially the second and third columns of the table, p. 337.

(2) The same type in different regions or countries (e.g., Italian and French opera)

(3) The same type in different idioms (e.g., polyphonic and homophonic chanson)

(4) The same type in different media (e.g., the piano and organ sonata)

c. The style types and their sub- or related types may not always offer full differentiations, with resultant overlapping (e.g., folksong, folklike song, "art" song). All of the types and their sub- or related types are, nevertheless, stylistically distinguishable as entities, through sufficiently sharp style analysis.

[32 d. Examples of the chief style types and, in important instances, of sub- or related types, are listed below; the list is not exhaustive:[28]

Examples of the Style Types

I. TYPES

1. Anthem (cf. Motet)

2. Ballet

3. Canon (form name)

[32d

4. Cantata, for chorus, with or without soloist(s), and instrumental accompaniment (less extensive than an Oratorio; see Oratorio *54* and *54c*)

5. Cantata, solo (see Opera Derivations *53c*)

6. Canzona, polyphonic in-

II. SUB- OR RELATED TYPES

a. Comédie ballet
b. Symphonic ballet
a. Rota, Rondellus
b. Caccia
c. Chace
d. Round
e. Catch

a. Church cantata
  Protestant

[28] For full discussions of the types and for indications of their sub- or related types, especially the historical and regional, see *ibid.*, under the appropriate articles.

138

strumental (see Ricercar
65e)

7. Canzona, polyphonic
vocal (see Chanson *13*)
8. Canzona, homophonic
(see Song *75*)
9. Capriccio, polyphonic
(see Ricercar *66b*)
10. Capriccio, homophonic
(cf. Character piece 15)
11. Chaconne (see Variation   *a.* Passacaglia
83b)
12. Chanson, monophonic
(see Song *73*)
13. Chanson, polyphonic   *a.* Canzona, polyphonic (see
                                      Canzona *7*)
                                 b. Lied, polyphonic (see
                                   Lied *40*)

[32d
14. Chanson, homophonic
(see Song *75*)
15. Character piece[29]   *a.* Set of character pieces
16. Chorale-prelude   *a.* Chorale-variation
                                   b. Chorale-phantasy
17. Clausula   *a.* Double, triple, etc.,
                                   concerto
                                   b. Sinfonia concertante

18. Concerto, solo
19. Concerto grosso
20. Conductus
21. Dance types[30]
22. Divertimento   *a.* Serenata
                                   b. Cassation
23. Entr'acte (see Inter-
mezzo *35*)
24. Entr'acte, comédie ballet
(see Ballet *2a*)

[29] For typical titles, see Willi Apel, *ibid.*, ''Character piece,'' pp. 132-133.
[30] For the varieties, see Willi Apel, *ibid.*, ''Dance music,'' pp. 199-201.

25. Fantasia, polyphonic
(see Ricercar *66c*)
26. Fantasia, work in
"free" form
27. Frottola
28. Folksong   *a.* Folklike song (cf. Song
                                75)

29. Fughetta (see Fugue
30b)
30. Fugue   *a.* Double, triple, etc., fugue
                             b. Fughetta (a fugue with
                                limited exploitation)

31. Group-names (see In-
strument-group names
37, and Voice-group
names *85*)
32. Hymn, monophonic
(plain chant)
[32d
33. Hymn, polyphonic or   *a.* Catholic polyphonic hymn
homophonic   *b.* Protestant chorale
                             c. Calvinist hymn
                             d. Anglican hymn

34. Incidental music to
drama
35. Intermezzo, instrumental
36. Intermezzo (see Opera
52d)
37. Instrument-group   *a.* String duo, trio, etc.
names, especially in   *b.* Wind duo, trio, etc.
chamber music   *c.* Piano trio, quartet, etc.
                             d. Duo, trio, etc., for . . .

38. Lauda, monophonic
39. Lauda, polyphonic
40. Lied, polyphonic (see
Chanson *13*)
41. Lied, homophonic (see
Song *75*)

42. Liturgic drama, mono-
    phonic (plain chant)
43. Lyric piece (cf. Charac- *a.* Short lyric
    ter piece 15)   *b.* Sustained lyric
44. Madrigal, polyphonic   *a.* Madrigal, semi-
                 polyphonic
                b. Glee, semi-polyphonic
                c. Ballet, semi-polyphonic

45. Madrigal, solo
46. Mass, monophonic (plain
    chant)
47. Mass, polyphonic   *a.* Plain chant mass
                b. Cantus firmus mass
                c. Parody mass
                d. Freely invented mass
                e. *A cappella* mass
                f. Requiem mass

[32d
48. Mass, for chorus, with *a.* Concert mass
    or without soloist(s), *b.* Requiem mass
    and instrumental accom-
    paniment
49. Melodrama, recitation-
    instrumental
50. Motet, polyphonic   *a.* Isorhythmic motet
                b. Chorale-motet

51. Music drama
52. Opera   *a.* Monody
                b. Madrigal opera
                c. Opera seria
                d. Intermezzo
                e. Opera buffa
                f. "Grand" opera
                g. Opéra comique
                h. Vaudeville
                j. Masque
                k. Ballad opera
                m. Singspiel
                n. Operetta

p. Chamber opera
q. Jazz opera
r. Musical comedy

53. Opera derivatives as
    independent types

    a. Overture
    b. Concert aria
    c. Solo cantata
    d. Scena

[32d
54. Oratorio, for chorus,
    with or without
    soloist(s), and instru-
    mental accompaniment

    a. Passion oratorio
    b. Concert oratorio
    c. Cantata (see Cantata 4)

55. Organum, Perotinian,
    etc.
56. Overture

    a. Opera: French overture
    b. Opera: Italian overture
    c. Music drama: Vorspiel,
       Prelude
    d. Overture (see Overture-
       suite 58)

57. Overture, concert
58. Overture-suite (cycle
    beginning with a French
    Overture)
59. Passacaglia (see
    Variation 83b)

    a. Chaconne

60. Part-song, homophonic
    (cf. Madrigal 44a-b)
61. Passion, monophonic
    (plain chant)
62. Passion, polyphonic
63. Passion, for chorus, with
    or without soloist(s),
    and instrumental accom-
    paniment (see Oratorio
    54a)
64. Prelude

    a. Independent piece
    b. With fugue, etc.

65. Rhapsody, work in

"free"form (see
Character piece *15*)

66. Ricercar, polyphonic

    a. Canzona (see Canzona *6*)
    b. Capriccio (see Capriccio *9*)
    c. Fantasia (see Fantasia *25*)

[32d

67. Rondo (form name)
68. Rota (see Canon *3a*)
69. Sequence, monophonic
(plain chant)
70. Sonata, solo (cycle)

    a. Descriptive sonata (e.g., Kuhnau)
    b. Sonata in one movement (coalescing of the cyclic divisions)

71. Sonata, solo with accompaniment

    a. Sonata, solo with basso continuo

72. Sonata, ensemble (cycle)

    a. Trio-sonata
    b. Sonata da camera (see Suite *77a*)
    c. Sonata da chiesa

73. Song, monophonic
(Troubadour, Trouvère, etc.)

    a. Rondeau
    b. Virelai, Chanson balladé
    c. Ballade, Bar, Canzo
    d. Lai

74. Song, with polyphonic accompaniment

    a. Rondeau
    b. Virelai, Ballata
    c. Ballade

75. Song, homophonic

    a. Chanson (see Chanson *14*)
    b. Canzona (see Canzona *8*)
    c. Lied (see Lied *41*)
    d. Air
    e. Ballad
    f. Folklike song (cf. Folksong *28a*)
    g. Song cycle

76. Suite, solo (cycle)

    a. Ordre
    b. Partita
    c. Lesson

[32d
77. Suite, ensemble (cycle)

    a. Sonata da camera
    b. Overture-suite (see Overture-suite *58*)
    c. Symphonic suite
    d. Program suite

78. Symphonic poem, tone poem
79. Symphony (cycle)

    a. Program symphony
    b. Choral symphony
    c. Chamber symphony
    d. Symphony in one movement (coalescing of the cyclic divisions)

80. Toccata, polyphonic
81. Toccata, homophonic
82. Transcription, virtuoso
83. Variation (form name)

    a. Dance with double, etc. (see Dance types *21*)
    b. *Ostinato* (see Passacaglia *59*; Chaconne *11*)
    c. Chorale-variation (see Chorale-prelude *16a*)
    d. Partita (see suite *77*)
    e. Symphonic variation

84. Villanella
85. Voice-group names

    a. Vocal duet, trio, etc.

D. *The History of Style*

33. A PHASE OF THE HISTORY OF MUSIC

a. The history of style is a central factor in the history of music.

b. The history of style is the subjective reflection of the factual and objective history of music.

34. THE DYNAMIC OF STYLE HISTORY

a. Reconcilable opposition among the components of style, rather than conformity, marks points of greatest distinction in style history; e.g., Bach: polyphonic independence *vs.* harmonic coördination; Mozart: structural rationalism *vs.* incipient romantic warmth; Beethoven: classic bases of structure *vs.* individualism of ideas and their dynamic treatment.

b. The product of the controlled tensity of such oppositions is vitality and originality of style [6a(3d); 42f(8)]

35. THE CONTINUITY OF STYLE HISTORY

a. The history of style is indivisible: the larger identity of style transcends the apparent parts.

b. The history of style is a cumulative and unifying account of the successive style epochs and their subdivisions, through—

    (1) Reconstruction of the data, through—

        (a) Historical scholarship
        (b) Historical imagination

    (2) Analysis of the data

    (3) Synthesis of the data

    (4) Interpretation of the data

c. The history of style (and hence in part the history of music) is the product of sustained style criticism[31] [28-42]

36. PRACTICAL APPROACHES TO THE HISTORY OF STYLE

¶1 Style may be considered from any or several of its numerous facets, e.g.,

[31] For the fusion of historical interpretation and style criticism, observe Paul Henry Lang, *Music in Western Civilization*, New York, 1941.

a. The phenomena of change

b. Proliferation of the orders and types of style

c. The phenomena of pattern

d. The career of individual elements of pattern (e.g., the history of melody, the history of texture)

e. The phenomena of expressive effect

f. The aesthetic pattern of the history of style

g. Individualistic composers as the creators of style and style history

etc.

37. STYLE ACROSS THE ARTS

a. Style is related to, and affords the chief link with, the history and aesthetics of the other arts.

b. This relation is borne out by the substantial community of concepts, terminology, and aesthetic and critical thought among the arts.

V. The Criticism of Style

A. Conceptions of Style Criticism

38. DIVERSE OBJECTIVES OF STYLE CRITICISM

¶1 Different views of the function of style criticism range from the scientifically objective to the idiosyncratically personal. A composite point of view may obtain. The following are some approaches: style criticism as—

a. A tool of examination and analysis

b. An instrument in investigating the history of music

c. A contribution to the restoration of the style of a composition, composer, or epoch, through scholarship and historical imagination

d. An aesthetic epitome of a case or problem [41]

e. A contribution to aesthetic thought

f. An avenue to the refinement and security of musical perception and taste

g. A form of artistic self-expression

h. A socio-artistic commentary

j. A discipline
etc.

39. DIVERSE APPROACHES TO THE DETERMINATION OF VALUE

¶1 The following are conventional attitudes in the determination of value [42f]:

a. Judgments by fixed standards, presumably traditional or arbitrary

b. Subjective appraisal by intuition and personal feeling according to individual criteria (cf. the perceiver's pleasure) [8j]

c. Objective appraisal by the assembling and sifting of data and by objective diagnosis

¶1 Criticism without evaluation[32]

d. Mixtures (to some extent unavoidable and sometimes useful)

B. Procedures in Style Criticism

40. THE EVIDENCES OF STYLE

a. The evidences introduced in style criticism are determined selectively for the case or problem in hand from several or many of the aspects of style set forth throughout this *Handbook;* see especially [30-32]. A scheme or formula may be constructed, suited to any given case or problem, and conforming to the objectives and procedures chosen. [38, 41-42]

b. The distinctive conjunction of components, and the distinctive emphasis among them, reveal style. [1]

41. THE APPLICATIONS OF STYLE CRITICISM

¶1 Applications vary according to the focus. or subject of the criticism, e.g.,

a. The *style case,* ranging from the individual composition to the epoch, calls for consideration of the following:

(1) Historical orientation [28; 33-35]
(2) Antecedents of the given style
  (a) Precedents
  (b) Influences received
    1. Direct (discipleship)
    2. Indirect (forerunners)

[32] See Morris Weitz, ''Criticism without Evaluation,'' in *The Philosophical Review*, vol. 61, no. 1, Jan. 1952.

(3) The contemporary context of the style
  (a) Status of music and composers
  (b) Conventions of the time
    1. Notation practices
    2. Performance traditions and practices
  (c) Influences received
    1. Direct (discipleship)
    2. Indirect (background)
  (d) Relation to other styles of the time
(4) Consequents
  (a) Predictive implications
  (b) Influences passed on
    1. Direct (discipleship)
    2. Indirect (general)

[41 b. The *style problem*
  (1) Historical
  (2) Theoretical
  (3) Aesthetic
  (4) Interpretative (in performance)
  (5) Mixtures

42. THE PRACTICE OF STYLE CRITICISM

¶1 The exercise of style criticism is a form of applied aesthetics.

¶2 In illustration of the practice, the following procedure in dealing with the style of a composer or individual work is offered:

[42 a. Observation ⎫
    b. Description ⎬ of the pertinent phenomena
    c. Analysis ⎭

¶1 It is obvious that by no means all of the evidence taken into account will appear in the actual critique.

d. Consideration of the historical context [33-37]

e. Synthesis of the evidence into essential generalizations, using the guidance offered by the marks of style [30]

f. Practical evaluation of this synthesis and of the auditory experience, in the case of a composer's work or works

¶1 Evaluation involves consideration of both pattern and expressive effect and their synthesis in style, and will take into account:

(1) Craftsmanship
(2) Quality of the thematic ideas
(3) Logical conviction of the pattern
(4) Style homogeneity
(5) Mood interest and stimulation
(6) Quality of imagination ⎫
(7) Creative vitality ⎬ [6a(3d)]
(8) Originality ⎭
(9) Artistic sincerity [6a(3e)]
(10) Impressiveness of the comprehensive expressive effect
(11) Aesthetic distinction
(12) Aesthetic conviction
(13) Taste
(14) Durability (the test of time; its absence not determinative)
(13) The larger artistic conviction as a whole

g. Comparison of the style examined with other styles, including those of other arts

C. The Style Critic

43. THE ENDOWMENT OF THE STYLE CRITIC

a. Musical experience
b. Intellectual insight
c. Learning
d. Historical imagination
e. A sense of relation
f. Aesthetic sensitivity and insight

g. Taste (a product of education through the exercise of criticism)

h. Catholicity in temperament and taste

j. Objectivity

k. Literary skill

m. Critical experience

INDEX OF CHIEF TOPICS AND IDEAS

in their chief locations

¶1 Lowercase Roman numerals refer to pages at the front.

¶2 References in [ ] apply to the analytically marked topics and subtopics of the *Handbook*.

¶3 Various terms not entered in the INDEX will be found treated in the text under the more comprehensive topics which include them (e.g., ''rondo,'' under forms, integral, linear; ''development,'' under thematic functions; etc.)

¶4 Some topics included in the INDEX may be found to receive slight attention in the text. They are noted, nevertheless, because of the light that the context in which they are found throws on them, or on their classification as ideas.

Accent [3b(2a)*3, 5-7*]

accentuation, rising, falling [4a(2b) *1-2*; 4c (1d)]

——, inflection, structural [4c(1d)*1c*]

aesthetic emotion [8e¶1]

aesthetic experience [8h, j; 9a(4)]

aesthetic pace [5c(7)]

——, attributes of [5c(7h)]

——, consequence to expressive effect [5c(7g)]

——, field of [5c(7a)]

——, index to changing expressive effect [5c(7h)*5*]

——, qualitative character of [5c(7b)]

——, tensity in [5c(7c-f)]

aesthetic value [5c(11g)*1*; 8h(4)]

amodality, amodal systems [3b(1b)*3*]

anacrusis, rising accentuation [4a(2b) *1*]

analogy [5c(3)]

——, applications of, linear [5c(3c)*1a*]

——, applications of, polylinear [5c (3c)*1b*]

——, deferred [5c(3c)*2*]

——, graduated [5c(3b)*2*]

——, immediate [5c(3c)*1*]

——, in nuance [5c(3d)*4*]

——, in rhythm [5c(3d)*1*]

——, in tensity [5c(3d)*3*]

——, in thematic functions [5c(3d)*5*]

——, in tonality [5c(3d)*2*]

——, non-structural [5c(3d)]

——, relations of analogues to original [5c(3a)]

——, simple [5c(3b)*1*]

——, structural [5c(3a-c)]

artistic integrity [6a(3c); 42f (9)]

asymmetry, in structure [5c(4c)]

attention, fluctuation of, in accent [3b (2a)*3*; 3b(2b)¶1]

atonality, *see* amodality

augmentation, thematic mutation [4c (2d)*4*]

Balance, in linear structure [4c(1b)*1*; 4c(1d); 5c(3c)*1a(1)*]

balanced phraseology [3c(2)]

bass line, index of tonal or modal progression [4b(7b)*1a(2c)*; 4b(7b)*1b (2c)*]

basso continuo, in implied texture [3c (1c)*3*; 4b(5a); 15f(2)]

beats, in time relations [3b(2a)*1-6*]

Cadence [4c(1a)*2a*; 4c(2c)*2a*]

cadences, staggered, in polyphony [4c (2c)*2c*]

cantus firmus, structural procedure [4c (2h)*1*]

chord [4b(7a)]

chromatic [4a(1e)*2*; 4b(7a)*2a*¶2; 4b (7b)*1a2b*]

classic temperament [3d¶1; 3d(1)]

climax, structural [4e(eg)*7c*; 5c (7c) *3c*]

closed-ended, in linear structure [4c(1b) *1e*]

color, chromatic [3a(5b)]

——, organic [3a(5a); 3b(4a)*7*]

——, tone color or timbre [3a(5c); 3b (5)]

communication, expressive effect as [9]

——, nature of musical [9a]

comparison, by the perceiver [5b(1)]

composers cited, in illustration of forms [4c(1h)*3*; 4c(1j)*1-2*;4c(2h)*4*; 4c (2j)*3*; 4c(2k)*1d*]

——, in illustration of style epochs [28a (4)]

conjunct, contact of spans [4c(2b)*1d*]

consonance-dissonance [3b(4)¶1; 3b (4a); 3b(4b)*2-3*]

contra-integration, in progression [5c (6j)]

contrast [5c(5)]

——, basis in range and rate of change [5c(5a)]

——, extensive [5c(5b)¶1]

——, factors implementing [5c(5b-c)]

——, local [5c(5d)¶1]

criticism of style [38-43]

——, conceptions of [38]

——, procedures in [40-42]

cross-idioms, textural, phraseological [3c (3)]

cumulation, in integration [5c(6f)]

cursive, in linear structure [4c(1b)*2*]

cursive phraseology [3c(2)]

——, in polylinear structure [4c(2b)*1*]

cycle, the cyclic principle [4c(1j)¶1; 4c(3)]

——, in linear structure [4c(1j)]

——, in polylinear structure [4c(2k)]

Declamation, melodic [3b(2d)*1*; 4a(4d) *9*; 6b(2b) *3a(1)*]

decoration [4a(1f)*2*; 4b(6)]

definitions of terms, preliminary, page xi

delineation [6b(1c)*1*; 9b(1b)III]

description [6b(1c)*2*; 9b(1b)IV]

design, page xi; [2c; 10b; 11]

detensity, *see* intensity-tensity-detensity

diatonic [4a(1e)*1*; 4b(7b)*1a(2a)*]

diminution, thematic mutation [4c(2d) *4b*]

disjunct, contact of spans [4c(1b)*1c*]

dissonance, *see* consonance-dissonance

——, structural [5c(7c)*3e*]

drama, influence of, on pattern [6b (2b)]

dramatic [5c(7g)*2b*]

duodecuple amodality [3b(1b)*3b*]

duration, distinctions of [3b(2c)]

dynamic relations [3b(3)]

Eclecticism [3d(3); 16c; 16d(5); 24c; 25d]

empathy [8d]

equilibrium [5c(8)]

——, compensation of imbalances [5c (8a)]

——, degrees of compensation [5c(8b)]

ethos, in mode [3b(1a)*3*¶2]

ethos, pathos: aesthetic temperaments [3d¶1]

expectation, by the perceiver [5b(2)]

expression, expressive effect [2b; 7-8]

expressive effect, as communication [9]

——, as the perceiver's experience [7b-c]

——, consequence of aesthetic pace to [5c(7g)]

——, dramatic [5c(7g)*2b*]

——, lyric [5c(7g)*2a*]

——, lyrico-dramatic [5c(7g)*2c*]

——, source of [7]

extensity [5c(9)¶1; 5c(9b)*3*]

extent [5a(4); 5c(8)]

——, characterized by aesthetic pace and length [5c(9a)*2*]

——, characterized by temporal pace and length [5c(9a)*1*]

——, conformation to different criteria [5c(9j)]

——, field of, in progression [5a(4); 5c(9)]

——, graduation of [5c(9e)]

——, impulses generating [5c(9c)]

——, incorporated tensity [5c(9h)*2*]

——, indeterminate character of [5c (9f)]

——, intrinsic tensity [5c(9h)*1*]